HENRY PAOLUCCI

LECTURES ON

ROMAN HISTORY

Foreword by Anne Paolucci
Preface by Frank D. Grande

Library of Congress Cataloging-in-Publication Data

Paolucci, Henry.
Lectures on Roman history / Henry Paolucci ; foreword
by Anne Paolucci ; edited & preface by Frank D. Grande.
   p. cm.
"The material offered here is based on extensive often
verbatim notes by two students, Mr. George Bock and Mrs.
Helen Mann, who were students in the course on Roman
history offered at The City College of New York, in 1959"—
P. viii.
Includes bibliographical references.
ISBN 1-932107-06-1 (alk. paper)
1. Rome—History. I. Grande, Frank, D. II. Title.
DG209.P35 2004
937—dc22

                                    2004040583

Published for
THE BAGEHOT COUNCIL
by
GRIFFON HOUSE PUBLICATIONS
P. O. BOX 468
SMYRNA, DE, 19977

CONTENTS

FOREWORD

I am grateful to Dr. Frank D. Grande, friend and later, colleague of Henry Paolucci, who volunteered to edit this manuscript. The original text was the result of verbatim notes by two students who were in the course on the subject, offered at The City College, (CUNY). They are faithful and accurate; in them one recognizes the authority and general style of Professor Paolucci's writings, although there is also the spontaneity characteristic of classroom lectures.

The main attraction of *Lectures on Roman History*, in addition to its terse style, is the frequent interjection of contemporary references, judgments, and conclusions, in a way that is often "chatty." Among the most striking are those in which the *Pax Romana* is compared with the political realities of our day, especially the role of the United States in our updated global scenario. I am pleased to have had a part in making these lectures available to a wider audience.

ANNE PAOLUCCI
October 2003

PREFACE

In 1959, while pursuing my doctoral studies in history, I applied for an adjunct teaching position at Brooklyn College. The late Professor Harry Bernstein, who was then in charge of the evening session, called me to come in for an interview because he had a last-minute opening. I presented my curriculum vita and, as we began to talk, he asked whether I knew any of the faculty at Brooklyn. I responded that I had once briefly met Henry Paolucci. The name was like a *zauberwort*. Bernstein launched into a panegyric, telling me that Henry was one of the greatest teachers he had ever observed and lamented that there was no full-time position to offer him. Suddenly a bell rang. Bernstein glanced at his watch, exclaimed, "I'm going to be late for class!" and bolted toward the door. As he grabbed the doorknob, he whirled, pointed to me and said: "You know Henry — you're hired!"

Since my second class in the late afternoon ended just before Henry's first one began, I decided to sit in on his lectures and quickly saw why they were overflowing: students not only heard an original point of view, but a dynamic presentation as well. Twice a week, after his two classes were over, we would walk to the subway together and ride half the way home before parting. All this time we talked, questioned each other, and argued. It was a new education for me – a true Socratic dialectic. We kept in close contact after that, even when I served in the army and later went to Oxford University. In time, we became close friends. When he taught at St. John's University, I sat in on his courses in classical political theory, Hegel, and the history of political thought.

The material offered here is based on extensive notes taken by Mr. George Bock and Mrs. Helen Mann, who were students in the evening session course on Roman history offered at The City College of New York in the Spring of 1962. I have tried to preserve the integrity of their notes while making the material fully comprehensible to someone who never took the course. No attempt has been made to fill in areas not covered in the notes, areas which the instructor presumably expected the students to expand in their reading.

Professor Paolucci took Hegel's view of Roman history as his organizing theme and systematically pursued this throughout. In two areas in particular — the discussion of the impact of Hellenistic philosophies on educated Romans and the wide range of topics covered in the notes placed at the end (either "asides" or responses to students' questions) — Professor Paolucci's phrasing, as well as his ideas, comes through.

I cannot be certain what books the students were required to read or what editions may have been quoted from in class. But in order to ensure uniformity, I have given page references to scholarly and philosophical works from the following editions: Georg Wilhelm Friedrich Hegel, *The Philosophy of History*, tr. J. Sibree (New York: Dover Publications, 1956); Theodor Mommsen, *The History of Rome*, ed. Dero A. Saunders & John H. Collins (New York: Meridian Books, 1961); M. Rostovtzeff, *Rome*, tr. J. D. Duff, ed. Elias J. Bickerman (New York: Oxford University Press [Galaxy], 1963). For classical works, I have cited the book and chapter, which are standard in all editions.

FRANK D. GRANDE, D.PHIL(OXON)
September 2003
The City College, CUNY

LECTURES ON
ROMAN HISTORY

I. SOME BASIC CONCEPTS
GREEK BACKGROUNDS AND THE
THREE PHASES OF ROMAN HISTORY

There are some who are of the opinion that there is no particular reason why we should study the history of Rome after that of Greece. We might just as readily study both contemporaneously. Roman and Greek history were contemporaneous. Roman history on the Italian peninsula goes as far back in time as Greek history on the Greek peninsula. This point of view overlooks the fact that it is meaningless to study history until historical facts begin to exist. Until a people make history they will not write about it and it will not exist. Greece's recorded history began with the Persian Wars. The Romans made history and began to write about it with the Punic Wars and when they conquered the Greeks.

It is natural therefore to study the Greeks before the Romans since it was the Greeks who first made history. And it is natural to study the Romans after the Greeks since it is largely when they conquered the Greek world that they moved onto the stage of history. *It is necessary in studying peoples historically to take them in the order in which they became historical.*

According to Hegel all historical peoples go through three phases. In the first phase we find a people concentrating on one thing only and doing it well. In the second phase these people encounter another people who are very complicated and who are concentrating on many things, and they slaughter them. In the third phase the same people start concentrating on many things and become complicated, and they in turn run up against another people who

1

are concentrating on one thing only and are slaughtered by them. The cycle begins again.

In the third phase a people loses its political history and becomes essentially economical. Their function is to prepare the way for the world's next historical people. In considering the history of a people, historians usually stop before they reach the third phase.

Hegel, who wrote at length about the subject, knew at what point to introduce Roman history.

> The third period of the history of the Greeks brings us to their contact with the people which was to play the next part on the theater of the World's History; and the chief excuse for the contact was—as pretexts had previously been—the liberation of Greece. After Perseus, the last Macedonian King, in the year 168 B.C. had been conquered by the Romans and brought in triumph to Rome, the Achaean league was attacked and broken up, and at last in the year 146 B.C. Corinth was destroyed. Looking at Greece as Polybius describes it, we see how a noble nature, such as his, has nothing left for it but to despair at the state of affairs and to retreat into philosophy; or if it attempts to act, can only die in the struggle. In deadly contraposition to the multiform variety of passion which Greece presents—that distracted condition which overwhelms good and evil in one common ruin—stands a blind fate—an iron power ready to show up that degraded condition in all its weakness, and to dash it to pieces in miserable ruin; for cure, amendment, and consolation are impossible. And this crushing Destiny is the Roman power. (*Philosophy of History*, 277)

The first phase of Roman history from the beginning to about 146 B.C. is concerned with the overthrow of the Monarchy and the expansion of the Republic.

The second phase deals with the fall of the Republic from 146 B.C. to the death of Augustus in 14 A.D.

The third phase of Roman history is that of absolute equality under the democratic monarchy.

During the second phase of Roman history good

things had happened. Power was devolving down to the masses and being stripped from the upper classes. As the upper classes became progressively more impotent and unhappy, the broad base of the masses became happier and happier, until this inexorable downward push of power had all but extinguished anything superior to the masses. In the third phase under the democratic monarchy, everyone became equal as opposed to an aristocratic monarchy which supports class distinctions. The masses were now ecstatically happy but something terrible and unforeseen happened; the downward push of power devolved to the masses and crushed all Romans into equal meaninglessness. At the time of the Roman Empire, actually a democratic monarchy, everyone was equal and no one wanted to do anything, since there was no possible reward for doing it. People had to be forced to do things. The Roman story logically ends when everybody became a citizen no matter what he did or did not do.

In studying Rome we should begin with Polybius, the Greek, who casts the first light on the history of Rome about 146 B.C. This may appear to be rather late. Why should we begin then? Because it was then that Roman history was first written and it was then that it was first made. It is at this point that Rome enters the mainstream of history.

After Polybius the Romans began to write their history in a meaningful way. He taught them how to write history.

Polybius is among the most rewarding historians that one can read. To develop a good Roman historiography one must always begin with Polybius.[1] Polybius was the Greek who taught other peoples how to write history. One could not turn to Herodotus and Thucydides for instruction because they were Greeks writing for Greeks.

Polybius wrote about a period represented by innumerable incomplete records. Out of archeological debris and misleading legends he picked out what was essential. But how does one decide what is essential? Polybius gives us a criterion. He gives us the laws of growth of a civilization, laws which any civilization must inevitably follow.

Polybius confronted a mass of material extracted from the Roman past, fragments of documents and legends, materials exhumed from the archeologist's most lucrative source — ancestral tombs. But he knew that one can never find a people's history in tombs; only boasts can be found there. Even the Romans did not take the inscriptions of their tombs seriously. They knew that the stories left there were frauds, boasts contrived to impress posterity. Polybius surmised however that if one compares enough boasts, in time the fictions will cancel themselves out and an outline approaching something like the truth will emerge. In viewing the only extant relics of the Roman past, Roman boasts and legends, Polybius applied to them the characteristic fruit of Greek genius which enabled him to select the essential from the non-essential; he applied the universal idea.

The big question that Polybius asked was, "How could a power that had almost been obliterated by Hannibal resurge within 54 years to dominate the entire world?" To answer this question, he asks us to consider two separate factors: that which is universal and that which is particular about the Romans.

Polybius looked at Rome and asked first what was universal about Rome that could be applied to any civilization. He did not ask "What is it that is uniquely Roman?" This is the scientific approach to history. Science must first discover what is universal. Polybius does what every scientist does. He probes the general nature of the object of his study. What, Polybius asks, is the general form of any government that has ever existed or will ever exist?

He concedes that the universal idea has already been worked out:

Now the natural laws which regulate the merging of one

form of government into another are perhaps discussed with greater accuracy by Plato and some other philosophers. But their treatment, from its intricacy and exhaustiveness, is only within the capacity of a few. I will therefore endeavor to give a summary of the subject, just so far as I suppose it to fall within the scope of a practical history and the intelligence of ordinary people.

The cycle which Polybius outlines is simple. He says in effect that if man and his civilization were almost completely wiped out, it would inevitably follow that those who survive would form an entourage behind the strongest, most dynamic personality, in very much the same way as animals would herd about a leader. And should there be more than one of these leaders there would be an inevitable locking of horns, since there can only be one leader, one plan of action. That this is so and that it would override any feelings of kinship is illustrated by Romulus and Remus and by Pompey and Julius Caesar, brothers, brothers-in-law and enemies.

Polybius goes on:

. . . as with the animals, he who was superior to the rest in strength of body or courage of soul would lead and rule them. For what we see happen in the case of animals that are without the faculty of reason, such as bulls, goats, and cocks—among whom there can be no dispute that the strongest take the lead—that we must regard as in the truest sense the teaching of nature. Originally then it is probable that the condition of life among men was this—herding together like animals and following the strongest and bravest as leaders. (VI. 5)

What happens to the leader now depends on how successful he is. If he is a successful leader, respected by his followers, he will lead or rule with authority and his rule develops into kingship. If he rules purely by strength and not by the consent of his followers, he will remain a despot. When the respected king passes on, it will be natural for his power to be transferred to his sons. The people will reason that the sons should most probably have some of his qualities. As the kingship is thus passed along, the need for the "king" will diminish. He will not be called upon to fight battles or save the city. Times will have changed. The people will look at him and wonder what it is about him that they should respect since he is doing nothing. The king, sensing this, will begin to demand respect since he can no longer earn it. When he begins to demand respect too violently he becomes a tyrant.

The universal factor for change in any government is the *devolution of power*. This is present in all governments and Polybius found it to be present in Rome.

The second thing Polybius points out is what is particular about Rome. That which is particular about Rome is that she has managed to arrest this process of devolution. Rome did not stop the process. Polybius maintains that this is impossible, but Rome slowed it down. How does one arrest the devolution of power? By realizing that the very thing one wants and achieves contains in it the germ of its own destruction. Aristotle in the fifth book of his *Politics* concentrated intensively on the causes of devolution. The very things which make some people happy inevitably make other people unhappy. (When a government satisfies the importer, it usually alienates the exporter.)

Polybius theorized that to arrest the process of devolution, it is necessary to realize that the state of government which one presently enjoys is not going to last forever. The aristocrats cannot be expected to keep on turning out beautiful and gifted children. They will produce ugly and stupid ones as well. One cannot count on being the best and staying the best forever. Having realized this, one must anticipate the next upcoming class, the next level of devolution of power, and make provision for it in the constitution.

The Romans established a mixed constitution. A mixed constitution implies a balance of powers, a system of checks and balances. There is a paradox here. If the universal pattern of devolution of power cannot, as Polybius claims, be stopped and one has a mixed constitution, does one really have a genuine system of checks and balances? For if one had a genuine balance of power, then one would have stopped the process of devolution and the universal principle of Polybius would have been invalidated. But when one realizes that a balancing of power is not a real balance, then in a mixed constitution one part of the government will inevitably dominate the other part. However, if the part that dominates makes clever concession to the other part, it will last longer, or stay the process of devolution. This is clearly what Polybius meant. *Though the devolution of power exists in all nations, in some, he maintains, it may be delayed.*

The Romans exemplified the theory of Polybius, but they did not do it through the process of reason; with them it was a process of natural growth. What did the Romans specifically do to arrest the devolution of power through checks and balances? Polybius distinguishes carefully what the Romans could do best. Their characteristic act was to know how to govern, to make laws. They do not try to explain themselves as do the Greeks; Virgil told the Romans what they were. He told them not to track the paths of the stars or try to breathe life into marble, but to rule, to preserve the peace with force, to lift up the lowly, to put down the proud. This was the mission of Rome.

Roman law was the great Roman contribution, the vehicle that expressed the meaning of Rome. If the Greek was asked what the vehicle of expression of his meaning was, he would point to the explanations of Thucydides, Aristotle or Plato; the Roman would point to his laws, for they represent exactly what the Romans did.

Polybius wanted to know why the Romans could beat the world. To understand the Romans he looked at their stories. Polybius did not go back beyond 390 B.C. This was a big date. Rome had suffered an almost total sack by the Celts. Anything documented before that date had been destroyed. All documents and ancient tales were written after 390 B.C.

To properly understand the Romans, it is necessary to discount all those things they shared in common with other peoples and to find out what it was about them that was purely theirs, that which made them unique. As an example, would it help to understand Germany if one knew that it had incorporated into itself the legacy of the Greeks, and Romans, and the medieval Church? The only way to really find out what Germany is, is to get the ancient stories of the Teutonic peoples that had not been touched by Greece, Rome and the Church. In finding out all the things that are not Greek, Roman and Christian, one extracts the seed which was nurtured by the humus of Greece, Rome and the Church. In like manner, to find out what is really English one must go back to the brutes of English litera-ture, beyond Chaucer, to the sources of the Arthurian legends.

How does one go about finding the seed of Rome that drew into itself the humus of the things about it? The Romans dug up for themselves the stories that character-ized them. If we were to neglect these stories, the only other approach would be to dwell on the geography of the Italian peninsula or to talk about the migrations which certainly must have occurred back there in the ancient beginnings of Rome. But we would have to say, with Hegel, when he was confronted with the work of Niebuhr (who started this kind of approach), that it is all very interesting, but what about Rome? We would still be no closer to finding out what the seed of Rome was.

The Romans told us the secret of why they were a legal people in their stories about their ugly beginnings. The Romans did not soft-soap their beginnings. It is neces-sary to know their stories to understand them. The secret is a very simple one. All nations have an ugly reality, but when one looks at their laws they are very handsome laws.

The Romans were the only people who have stories about their beginnings that are not hypocritical. How was Rome founded? The Roman would tell you. He would tell you that the founding father was a man who committed fratricide and the men that banded about him were outcasts from other tribes, bandits and thieves who had served time. The Roman would say that you can trust a man who has been in jail to have courage. The Romans' ugly reality was told in their legends and stories. But they were the only people, not only to have an ugly reality, but also to have ugly laws. They were doubly ugly. They were honest about it.[2] The Romans avoided the embarrassment of a contradiction between law and reality. When they said something they meant it. If they said a man could run for an office, then he could run for it. Therefore, it took a long time before they got around to saying it, and they did not say it often. But when they said it, they meant it.

The rights of the Romans as expressed in their laws were the result of a constant war between the haves and the have-nots. But it was not a real war. Had it been real, any stronger neighbor could have walked in and taken over. The Romans, plebs and aristocrats, had a deal and it was simply this: "I'll fight him harder than you will and you will have to admit that you need me."

The plebs rejected any cooperation with the ruling class. They would not even cooperate to beat the enemy. The two classes competed to beat him. There was constant rivalry among them as they tried to prove to each other how indispensable they were. They competed so violently that they took the known world.[3] This is why Rome was able to conquer the Mediterranean lands, half of Europe, and the Near East in 54 years.

II. THE FIRST PHASE

**THE OVERTHROW OF THE MONARCHY AND
THE EXPANSION OF THE REPUBLIC TO THE
DESTRUCTION OF CARTHAGE IN 146 B. C.**

After Polybius, when the literary people of Rome became proud, they tried to connect themselves to the Greeks. In Italy almost every city claimed Trojan origin. The Roman stories of their descendency from Trojans can never be clarified by archeology, for these stories refer to the beginnings and beginnings are not supposed to be clear. They speak of Aeneas and the gods and how the gods cautioned him against being like wily Ulysses and like wrathful Achilles, but instructed him to be pious and to do his duty. But once Aeneas is out of the way, the Roman story gets back into character.

There was a woman, a vestal virgin, who mysteriously comes of child, a practice frowned upon by the Romans, though in this case the father happened to be Mars. The children, since Romulus and Remus were twins, were left exposed to die. But they did not die because they were found by a she-wolf who raised them as its own. The Romans did not call this animal a dove, but a wolf.[4] Everyone knows what a wolf is: ravenous, bloodthirsty, a thief, and the twins had the blood of a wolf running through their veins.

The twins grew up and formed a kind of club with outcasts and thieves banding with them. They, tired of city life, made for the rugged hills where they could lead a real man's life. Everything was going well until both of the twins wanted to become founding fathers. It is embarrassing when there are two and each of them wants to be the man responsible for everything. Livy, the boastful historian of Rome, tells us that the liar Romulus killed his brother Remus, and thus became the founder of Rome, the father of his country. This only illustrates how the Romans always respected laws since by law the older brother had precedence over the younger; and as in the case of twins, both of them being of the same age and neither having legal precedence over the other, it was obviously necessary, in order that only one might give the orders, that one should kill the other, on legal grounds.

Romulus went on to build a kind of social and athletic club for the gang, and in his lifetime he developed from a gang leader to almost a king. But his was an odd gang. There were no women in it. This in itself suggests that the club had no future. So the gang members decided to ask some of the neighboring tribes for women, but the neighboring towns would have no part of Romulus and his boys. The men in those towns were well-behaved. They lived with their women in families and clans, were respectable and worshipped the gods. No one would give a daughter in marriage. Romulus and the club decided to give a ball in honor of a local god, and they invited everybody to come, even the girls. So the Sabines came with their wives and daughters. In the midst of the party, at a given signal, the Romans made off with the women.

This is an interesting story. If a later Roman patrician were ever to get too big, someone might remind him who his ancestors really were – thieves and rapists.

The Roman gang started out entirely on a legal basis. Theirs was a legal relationship. The members were all equal. The father owned all the offspring that came of his own body until they became contractual citizens. Until then he could sell them, or kill them if he liked.

Romulus is credited in these stories with having divided his gang into three tribes. However, since the gang prior to the Sabine incident had no women, the tribes were distinguished not by the blood of kinship, but rather by the tasks and functions which were designated to them. Romulus began his career as a despot. According to Polybius, if a despot rules well the people will reward his merit. What does it mean to reward merit? It means a division into classes. Roman history refers to the class distinction between patricians and plebeians as stemming from the rewards given to Romulus by his grateful people.

In our society the stress is not on class distinction but on the destruction of class distinctions. It must be remembered that Romulus, as the founder of any new state, destroyed old distinctions, just as Napoleon destroyed the feudal distinctions of the Ancient Regime. But destroying class distinctions at the outset is not the end. It is the beginning of the leveling process which clears the ground and permits new distinctions to be made. The men who banded about Romulus, the exiled and escaped convicts, were people who had left their countries behind. They also left their distinctions behind. New class distinctions had to emerge after this initial leveling process, otherwise the state would be a classless tyranny.

Within the gang of Romulus distinctions emerged. There were the patricians and the plebeians. Between the patricians and the plebeians emerged a third class called clients. In this class a man who may have been less than the plebeian became more than the plebeian by being faithful to the patrician. In a framework such as this, the monarch will gradually come to balance his power by siding with the plebeians against the power of the patricians and the favoritism they show their clients.

Romulus had established a senate of elders, the patricians, who were the old timers in his gang. The plebeians did the productive works but they also, from the beginning, had the special duty to be the fighting class. The plebeians were fighting producers. They must be distinguished from the productive classes of other societies who are not fighters.

The Romans were a special kind of gang in that they were not grounded in typical family relations. From the beginning they were fighters. With the Sabine incident an important moment in Rome's growth was reached, for it was here that an amalgamation of two aspects of the Roman character occurs: Roman force was combined with Sabine piety for family.

After having achieved many miraculous things, Romulus disappeared into a cloud and became a god. He did not leave a hereditary monarchy. The monarchy that followed him was an elective monarchy. A hereditary monarchy is a peaceful monarchy. It arises in a state when a people know what they want and what they want is best implemented by a hereditary succession of power. An elective monarchy, on the other hand, is tumultuous and is achieved only at the expenditure of great personal energy.[5]

The men that immediately followed Romulus were given short tenures of office. There was hesitation to confer the office of Romulus on any individual. As the next king, Numa was elected and he re-established the state on a new basis, that of religion. The practice of religion was made to conform to the laws of force on which the state had been founded. Religion solemnized these laws, and made them absolutely binding on the Roman conscience. Underlying everything the Romans did was the religious oath to uphold the state.

Livy characterizes the rule of the second king, Numa, as a new founding of the city. What had been established by Romulus, by force of arms, was sanctified by Numa on the basis of laws and morals. Hegel says of the force of arms with which Rome was founded that, "It is this peculiarity in the founding of the State which must be regarded as the essential basis of the idiosyncrasy of Rome. For it directly involves the severest discipline, and self-sacrifice to the grand object of the union. A state which had first to form itself, and which is based on force, must be held together by force."[6] (*Philosophy of History*, 284)

Numa founded religion on a basis secondary to the
state. As Hegel describes it:

> To the second king, Numa, is ascribed the introduction
> of the religious ceremonies. This trait is very remarkable
> from its implying that religion was introduced later than
> political union, while among other peoples religious
> traditions make their appearance in the remotest peri-
> ods and before all civil institutions. (*Philosophy of History*,
> 296)

The major deity of Numa was the god of boundaries.[7] Numa, with the inspiration of a beautiful nymph
who gave him advice from the gods, divided the land
among the people so that they owned it in their own right.
Under this Sabine king's rule the Romans enjoyed a period
of peace. It was a trait of Roman expansion, and of the
Roman kings, that an interval of aggression was followed
by an interval of peace. This was the continuous pattern of
Roman history. This was how Rome grew.

The third Roman king, Tullius Hostilius, brought
Rome into contact with the tribe of Albans. The Albans
were betrayed, and after the city of the Albans had been
razed in the tradition of Romulus, the Albans were given a
hill to live on.

The fourth king, Ancus Marcius, the grandson of
Numa, was, like Numa, a nice fellow. He was not aggres-
sive. All the time the Roman gang continued to grow. The
best way to understand Rome is to read the Kefauver
committee report on juvenile delinquency. The Romans,
in the best tradition of juvenile gangs, made everybody
they captured a member of the gang. Their creed was join
us or we'll bust you. They grew and became hard to rule.

From another gang, a fellow of a Greek father and
an Etruscan mother, Tarquinius Priscus saw that all the
conquered enemies of Rome were made members, so he
thought he would volunteer for membership.

His credentials qualified him. The Etruscans were
regarded as successful pirates by the Carthagians, who had

been at it for centuries. Tarquin the Elder liked Rome. It was a town that welcomed strangers. He brought in his wealth and rebuilt and beautified Rome.

His successor, Servius Tullius, redefined the tribes and mixed the factions to realign power. But because of the increasing benefits he lavished upon the people, he aroused the hatred of the gang of nobles. The people were satisfied with their king and, as the approving common will expanded, the king had less and less to do. Everything was running smoothly under his subordinates. It is at this point that the subordinates, the governors, began to question his authority. When the governors begin to feel the king is superfluous and they can run things without him, the king must do what the Pharaoh did in Egypt during the feudal periods, and what Abraham Lincoln did when the states began to assert their rights too strenuously; he has to go beyond his rebellious henchmen and get the support of his people. This he did through benefits and public works. He also attempted to nullify the strength of the nobles by packing the aristocracy with his own men. But increasing the number of nobles did not necessarily prevent the nobles from entertaining the idea that they did not need the king.

It was under the mask of a noble that the seventh and final king, Tarquin the Proud, descended from Tarquin the Elder, came into power. With the aid of the gang of nobles, he assassinated Servius Tullius. Tarquin the Proud then married the daughter of the assassinated king and made his wife a monster by compelling her to ride over the dead body of her father in a chariot. With Tarquin the Proud, an institution which had begun in despotism and flourished as kingship now became a tyranny.

Tarquin coped with the assembly of the nobles, the Senate, in another way than that of his predecessor who had stacked the Senate to weaken it. But what guarantee is there that, when there are 300 senators instead of the original 100, these 300 might not become stronger instead of weaker? This would particularly happen if the new senators took their nobility seriously. What do you do with senators who really want to be senators? Tarquin depleted the Senate.

Tarquin the Proud, once he had power, reduced the Senate of nobles to insignificance and he went over their heads to the people. The aristocrats knew that they could never beat a man backed by the people, unless they could somehow alienate the people from him. Has not the Republican Party devoted its best minds to devising some way of alienating the people from the democrats? While the king continued his policy of public works and benefits, his opponents were powerless. They had to create an unfavorable image of the king and his family. Now a propagandist against tyranny, Junius Brutus, emerged.

The king's son, Sextus, was involved in an immoral act and discrediting stories about the king's family were spread. Who wants an immoral king? The king was expelled.

Livy observes that had the Romans disposed of kingship too soon, the state would have never lasted. It would have been unwise to get rid of the king before his job was completed. But when the king's job is done and he is superfluous, and he knows that he is superfluous, the occasion arises for the most beautiful revolution. How superfluous poor Louis of France was, and knew he was, as he sneaked to the border of his country to escape, only to be whisked back by the French people who had to keep reminding him that he was their king!

The Romans did not want a king, but they wanted to keep his office. So they elected two 'kings' with equal powers, each acting as a balance on the other.

The big question raised by the monarchic period is, what is to be made of the legendary stories that represent it?[8] Some people have dismissed them as purely myth. Others have written plays about them. Most historians have tried to pull out of these stories some account of the nature of the institutions of government and powers of the people of this early phase of Roman history.

The legends of early Rome give us the major words which describe the constitution of that period. They tell us that the king had the imperium, which means that he had the ultimate coercive power in the state. A society which is based on force, as was Rome, needs such an office. This power was symbolized by the procession of lictors, who preceded the king carrying the symbol of the imperium, the fasces, a bundle of rods bound together around two axes. The bound rods represented the unity of the state. One represented the civil power of the king to rap the knuckles of his subjects when they threatened the unity of the state by overstepping their bounds. The other signified the military power the king could wield against the state's external enemies.

The word "fascism" is derived from this, but the emblem has also been engraved on American coins. The legends also introduce us to the Roman Senate and the people, Comitia Curiata.

From the beginning, in Rome's earliest legends we find the king, the senate and the curiata. These legends remind us that in Rome, a state established by force, there was initially nothing below the plebeian military class.

Machiavelli made quite a bit out of these early stories, basing his political writing heavily on the first ten books of Livy which contain the stories of the founding fathers of Rome. These legendary stories of Rome, whatever their historical significance, made quite a politician out of Machiavelli.

With the overthrow of the tyrant Tarquin, Roman history for most historians ceases to be legend and begins to become historical. To this period belongs the first historic Roman document, as recorded by Polybius, the Treaty of 509 between Rome and Carthage.

This was also about the time that Cleisthenes broke up the factions in Athens. Cleisthenes unified the three great warring classes of Athens by dividing them into ten new tribes. By dividing the old classes into ten parts and allowing each part to take the helm of government for a limited time, it became necessary for each party to resolve its internal differences. If the traditional factional disputes within the new tribe were not put aside, nothing would get done. Cleisthenes' realignment of classes, which brought to Athens a common will through division, was an expression of the creative genius of the Greeks. This approach would not have worked everywhere. It was possible only in a liberal society. In a strongly disciplined society men would die before they would abandon their class. The innovations of Cleisthenes were to be of prime importance later in the struggle of Athens against Persia. It gave to Athens a unity without which she would have perished.

The struggle of the Eastern Greeks with Persia was paralleled in the west by the struggle of the Sicilian Greeks against Carthage. The treaty between Rome and Carthage in 509 was a concession to the growing power of the Greeks in the west. It provided that between Rome and her allies and Carthage and her allies there should be peace. It was a nice mutual defense pact which almost exclusively favored Carthage. In the impending conflict with western Greece, Carthage wanted Rome to be on her side. *This treaty brings us safely into Roman documentary history.*

After Tarquin had been expelled from Rome, he solicited the aid of a foreign power in a bid to be restored to his rule. It seemed to be in the interest of Etruria to restore the tyrant, just as it was in the interest of England to try to restore to France the monarchy of the Bourbons. But Tarquin did not succeed.

The conflict that ensued between the Etruscans, who were trying to re-establish Tarquin, and the Romans, provided several memorable stories. There is the story of the heroic Roman, Horatius, who, behaving as if he were in a British film, held off the enemy single-handed while his panic-stricken men destroyed the bridge leading to Rome.

There is the story of Mucius Scaevola ("left-handed") who entered the Etruscan camp alone and tried to kill the king. When he was captured and the Etruscans were about to begin brain-washing him, he deliberately put his right hand into a fire and held it there to show them how much punishment he could take. The king was so impressed that he released the prisoner.

The beginning of the Republic was a period of great conflict. The important thing to notice is that as soon as the aristocrats of Rome had expelled the King and won, it became apparent to the populace that although the aristocrats had made great sacrifices to bring about this victory, they had better means with which to make them. The aristocrat had his followers, the clients, and wealth, whereas the plebs were just poor farmers and cattle raisers. When they were not being ravaged by war they were ravaged by famine. The plebs became aware that they were now in a worse condition than when they were ruled by a king. The king had, in the past, aligned himself with the plebs against the aristocrats; now they had lost their protector. They had lost all voice in the government, had no share in the administration, and the aristocrats would not willingly allow them to regain it. It became apparent that the revolution was in the interest of the artistocrats.

The Roman aristocracy had at first rallied everyone to their side against the king. But once he was expelled and they had time to formulate a positive policy, they began to suppress the very people who had helped to make the revolution possible.[9] The Roman aristocrats began to "conserve"after their revolution. They knew that it was impossible to conserve if they were to keep on making concessions to the plebs. They had exercised justice and moderation only until the dread of Tarquin and his allies subsided. Then the patricians began to tyrannize the plebs and slaves.

The reaction of the plebs took the form of "strikes" which were to re-occur during a long period of devolution of power. The plebs were primarily military men; they were not lovers of justice. If the stories the Romans wrote about themselves are examined carefully, it will be seen that no one regarded what he was doing as right, but what he could get away with.

The plebeians struck, demanding someone who would give them a voice. The two consuls who had been set up by the aristocrats were ineffective. To ease this situation a new office emerged, that of a man like Cromwell emerged, the dictator who could check the demands of the aristocrats. The abuses of the aristocrats had been due to their disunity. The dictator was a man who would stand above the factions. His function was to force upon all the people the tasks that must be done. He was a man who straddled both classes.

The dictator differed from the two consuls in that whereas they had had 12 lictors each, he had 24, and when he was in power all other magistrates were at once deprived of power. He was given this power for six months. The Athenians had the same kind of institution, an elected tyrant, a man involved in both factions who had not only the power but the right to make legislative changes without the consent of the government.

The Senate had appointed a dictator. But the dictator opposed the Senate and he was forced to quit the office. The dictator had tried to help the people and even though he failed, the people applauded him. The Senate was apprehensive. The peoples' favorite had been deposed. If the army, which was then still in the field, was disbanded and returned to the city, it might begin to conspire with the plebs. The army, however, had sworn allegiance to the consuls. With the dictator gone, it would still be bound by its oath. The Senate pretended a new war was breaking out and the army was ordered to remain in the field. For a time the disgruntled plebeian soldiers thought of killing the consuls. But they were dissuaded from this by the argument that no religious obligation could be discharged by a criminal act. It is significant that these people listened to the argument and were moved by it. They did have a common will for Rome. But they also felt that they were being abused. This is the worst kind of abuse — when someone who is willing to cooperate is taken advantage of. The plebeians retired in protest to the sacred mountain.

Why did the Senate come to terms with the plebeians? Livy observes that the Senate dreaded the people. He writes:

> In the city there was great panic; everything was at a standstill because of mutual apprehensions. The plebeians left behind feared violence from the senators, who in turn feared the plebeians remaining in the city, uncertain whether they should prefer them to stay or leave. "How long," they asked, "will the crowd of seceders remain quiet? What will happen if foreign war should break out in the meanwhile? Certainly the only remaining hope is harmony in the citizen body, and harmony must be achieved by fair means or foul."

This was the source of the Roman civil rights program. Who in their right mind would have made concessions otherwise?

At this point M. Agrippa came to reason with the plebeians and the senate made its first concession. *The plebeians got the right to elect tribunes.* The senate had two consuls and now gave to the plebeians two tribunes who had an inviolable negative power.

Livy describes the incident of Menenius Agrippa, a patrician with a conscience, who went to the camp of the striking plebs and tried to dissuade them from striking. His argument, according to Livy, went as follows:

> Once when a man's parts did not, as now, agree together but each had its own program and style, the other parts were indignant that their worry and trouble and diligence procured everything for the belly, which remained idle in the middle of the body and only enjoyed what the others provided. Accordingly, they conspired that the

hands should not carry food to the mouth, nor the mouth accept it, nor the teeth chew it. But while they angrily tried to subdue the belly by starvation they themselves and the whole body became dangerously emaciated. Hence it became evident that the belly's service was no sinecure, that it nourished the rest as well as itself, supplying the whole body with the source of life and energy by turning food into blood and distributing it through the veins. (2.32)

The argument of Agrippa likens the aristocrat to the stomach of the body, and the plebeians to the limbs, the fighting arms of the body. If the arms, resenting that the food they give the mouth goes to the stomach, refuse to give the mouth food, they will starve the stomach but also themselves. It then becomes apparent that the true function of the stomach is not to hoard the food for itself, but to send nourishment to the other parts of the body.

Plato expressed this organic view of society in his *Republic*, with his distinctions of the ruler, the fighter and the producer, each doing his task to support the entire body of the state. But Agrippa's image is much more superior, more expressive of this organic idea. Who were the plebs? They were the fighting arms of Rome, and the aristocracy was the stomach which nourished them.

The plebs felt that the fruits of their labor went somewhere else, to that aristocratic stomach, to the selfish few who just cut coupons.[10]

The Senate became conscious of the need to not alienate the class which sustained it. It began to flatter the plebeians in an effort to get their consenting will. However, flattery is a delicate skill. Not everyone is qualified to use it. There emerge two types of senators, the one who can successfully flatter the plebs and the one who cannot. Franklin Delano Roosevelt would have qualified as a patrician surpassing all patricians in the task of winning the will of the people.

The consuls, who were puppets of the Senate at

first, learned very quickly how to override the Senate. What could they do to surpass the Senate in power? Both consuls vied with each other to get the favor of the commoners. The people took a liking to the one who flattered them best.[11]

This effort to woo the plebeians finally disgusted the Senate and instead of two conflicting consuls they set up ten "consuls." Now, instead of having half the power, the consul had one-tenth. But the decemvirs ultimately usurped more power than the consuls. Whenever a need forces an innovation, it is bound to leave the innovator in a weaker position.

The decemvirs became tyrannical. The authority was not in the people but with ten nobles, who were limited neither by the tribunes, nor the other magistracies, nor the people. They forbade intermarriage and their administration was noted for corruption, cruelty and avarice. This imbalance of power cried injustice and caused a revolution. How were the decimvirs to be disposed of? How was Tarquin disposed of?

There was an immoral incident involving one of the decemvirs and a girl. The father stabbed his maiden daughter in the forum, to save her honor. This desperate father (and who could be a better leader for an uprising) ran to the plebeian troops who were at the time engaged in fighting a war. Upon hearing his story, they abandoned the war and, with the outraged father at their head, marched to Rome and took possession of the Sacred Mountain, on the Aventine Hill. The presence of the army enabled the Senate to pass a law which deposed the decemvirs. The decemvirs must have been beneficial to the people, they must have somehow bribed them with benefits (and what else is a benefit except bribery?), otherwise they would not have survived as long as they did. The people who have been bribed with kindness are the most indignant when they discover that their benefactor had his own interests really at heart.

The Senate was faced by the crowd that had made it possible to remove the decemvirs. What did they want? They wanted to know where they really stood and they wanted it in writing.

So the Twelve Tables, Rome's first laws, were written (traditionally, c. 450), and like Draco's code, they were very cruel laws. But first laws are always cruel. The Twelve Tables were terrible laws but they were true. A nation which has beautiful laws is lying.

The Twelve Tables imposed a host of capital sentences. Almost everything was punishable by death[12]. If a man was proved guilty of defrauding another, the defrauded party or parties had the right, should the convicted not correct matters, to slice his body into the respective number of pieces, one for each defrauded party, with full legal immunity to those who did the slicing.

Let no one say that there was no humor in the Twelve Tables.

The plebs had demanded a dictator and they got him. But he proved to be ineffective. They were then granted the privilege of electing two tribunes. In the tribunes they had the man who could not be touched by the patricians. The tribuneship was established about 493. As a spokesman of the plebs, the tribune had inviolable status. He could under no circumstances be taken from office. He could only be removed by election of the plebs. In this manner the power of the Senate was lessened. The state was now balanced between the Senate and the plebs. Whenever two powers achieve a balance, there invariably begins to emerge a third power.

When two classes struggle for power, the obvious solution is Marxian. The struggle will either eliminate the nation or it will produce a third class. How will this third class emerge? What will combine the patricians and plebeians into a third class? The fight for magistracies will combine them. When both parties have an equal right and are balanced in power, a third party comprised of the better people, a bureaucracy that really handles everything, will emerge. The third party will be the consul office, or the magistracy. The administration of the state will be carried on by the consul offices. The men that occupy these offices will not matter since the magistracies, because they will be so well organized, will function without them. What sort of a magistracy must it be in order that it will not be a tool of either party? A magistracy that is an end in itself, a professional administrative magistracy.

The Romans had opened up the administration to both classes. But there was the constant danger that the administration would become independent. Two balanced forces always give rise to a third new force. The problem for the Roman Senate was how to hold on to this tool, the joint administration, and make it completely its own.

One method the aristocrats employed to weaken the demands of the plebs, was to transfer some of the functions of the consular office, which was to become accessible to the plebs, to another office. After 450, the censor's office begins to emerge. Among the tasks of the censor were included taking a census of the population and assessing how much the citizens had in the way of property.[13] The censor assessed property to determine how much of the commonwealth was under the control of any given citizen. He determined who the people were that contributed the most to the commonwealth. A man will be concerned about the commonwealth in proportion to the extent that he controls or owns a part of it. The more a man owns of the commonwealth, the more he will care about what happens to it. The task of determining how much any man could say about the commonwealth fell to the censor.[14] The censor also determined the extent to which a man should contribute to the defense of the commonwealth. Obviously the man who would be expected to give most to the defense of the commonwealth would be the man who had most to defend. By determining what share the citizen had in the commonwealth, by assessing his property, the censor determined how much the citizen had to say about his government and how much he had to defend it.

In the beginning the Romans had been divided into three tribes. Servius Tullius instituted the reform of re-aligning the classes according to their property. The amount of wealth a man possessed put him into a particular class. But the original classes lost their meaning when their members lost their wealth. The tribes were aligned in such a way that the people who had the most to give to the commonwealth could vote on matters of state first and their vote was designed to carry greater weight. The aris-tocracy had priority in the voting process and it had the majority of available votes. But this natural advantage of the aristocracy could only be exercised when the nobles enjoyed solidarity. It was really a device to make clear whether there was solidarity among the nobles.

The patricians created the office of the censor. At first it looked so insignificant that the tribunes, who had the power to object to it, did not. The patricians had made concessions to the plebs, and the tribunes did not want to appear ungrateful by making an issue over such an insig-nificant office. This only exemplifies the many ways the upper class had of skinning a cat. It would not be too long before the office of consul would be open to the plebs. But by then the office of the censor would be almost confisca-tory in its power. When Cato was censor of Rome, the office had become the most important in the state.[15]

The only time concessions were made to the plebe-ians was when there was internal strife in Rome while a big job was being done by the people. All these concessions were made during a period of continual warfare, when the cooperation of the plebs was essential.

This is why Roman laws are true laws. They repre-sent genuine concessions coming from the upper class under duress.

The Canuleian law made marriage between the

classes possible. The plebs gained this advantage but in the spirit of a modern union leader; just so that no one would think the negotiations were completely closed, they suggested that the office of one of the consuls should be open to the plebs.

The plebs noticed that during wars it was the patricians who were promoted to higher military rank. But the plebs had many good soldiers, too, and they began to clamor for leaders that they could wholeheartedly follow, not men who had to pull rank to get obedience. The aristocratic military leader was not necessarily capable. Very often, as in most armies, the real leaders were his subordinates. These were the men who really commanded the respect of the troops and made things run smoothly, while the nominal leader was off base. The troops would dread when such a man, working under the delusion that he could actually command, would return to take matters into his own hands. Out of this situation emerged the military tribunes, a truly great concession to the plebs. The concession had to be made. The choice for the Senate was to be conquered by the enemy or by the Roman people.

The office of military tribunes elected by the plebeians to lead them was still filled by patricians. An incompetent aristocratic military leader is not always replaceable by his subordinates. Even when the plebs had achieved the legal right to elect a plebeian to lead them in battle, they did not dare exercise it. For about fifty years after being granted this right, the plebs still selected their leaders from among the aristocrats. If one failed, they would try another. The leaders of the plebs, the seemingly logical candidates for military tribunes, were noisy men gifted in the art of making the demands of the plebs heard. But who would dare entrust them with an important enterprise on which the life of everyone hung? They had that absolute unreasonableness required of a good union leader, but they would have been just as unsuccessful as military tribunes as Mike Quill would be at the head of a large corporation.

It took time to train the plebeians so that they could handle this job. One such man was Marius, who was prepared by an aristocrat. *The task of tutoring the plebs to lead themselves had to be done by the aristocracy.*

The class struggle continued until another concession was made, the Licinian Sextian law. This was a measure to rectify an imbalance in the economic situation, which was forcing many persons who had exceptional talent and would have made useful soldiers or statesmen, into debt and poverty. These men were the Mike Todd type of Roman, who were willing to make and lose a million without giving it a second thought. They were extremely useful to Rome, but their great failing was their ability to get into debt. When men of this caliber, through their indebtedness, were pushed into the servile class, a great danger to the security of the state arose. This very situation had almost ruined Athens when Solon finally moved to wipe it out. If a man is forced into the servant class and he is not really a servant, he is apt to cause all kinds of trouble for the state. The Licinian-Sextian law was a reshuffling of debts and a reallotment of lands to the citizens. The U.S. also followed this procedure with the western lands. It was necessary for the citizen only to stake his claim and make the land productive. In this reallotment of Roman lands, the big estates of the aristocracy were cut down. By this same law of 367, the plebs were definitely given the right to elect one consul from their own ranks. It also established honorific offices. These became very significant, as they do in all societies that eliminate class distinctions. The honorific office is enjoyed by the man who at dinner parties will deliver long speeches about equality and make very certain that he sits at the head of the table.

The patricians conceded to the plebs the office of consul, but at the same time they acted to restrict their power. They welcomed the plebeian consul, but they made certain to provide him with many assistants. Apart from the censor, they created the office of praetor urbanus, who was merely an insignificant secretary of urban affairs. What, however, were his powers? At first they were trivial, just another administrative office, just another magistracy among many magistracies. But because the powers were vague, they could be made to grow. The tribune, who was not a magistrate but who could have vetoed the formation of these magistracies, did not appreciate their full significance.

During the early period Rome had as its object the formation of a powerful common will. This is the problem of every state — to achieve a common will.[16] The degree to which it succeeds is measured by its common wealth. If it lacks a powerful common wealth, its common will is weak. The first task of the state is to develop a common will and then a common wealth. The great effort of Rome was to get a common will by destroying the private will. The whole object of Rome was to get all the Romans to will to do what Rome must do. Not to will to do it from the standpoint of a plebeian, or a patrician, but to make all the people willing.

Common will in a government enables a society to get things done to the extent that it has the consent of the governed. The greater the consent, the greater the common will. A great energy is released when wills are not working at cross purposes. A task which each nation in history has had to face has been to eliminate disagreeing wills and strengthen thereby its common will. But the task is not easy since the best way to achieve the common will is not by eliminating the wills that disagree, for these usually hold the rest together.

Before the founding father, there was no uniting will. When the founding father, the king, arrived on the scene, there was a uniting will, but to what extent do the citizens want to submit to it? At first only the king is willing to submit. Later the patricians give more of their wills to the common will.

This movement of a common will from the king through the patricians to the people is what is meant by the devolution of power. The whole danger of a devolution of power is that when the power devolves, the people to whom it has devolved want to chop off the parts from which it has devolved.

The Romans recorded every stage of this struggle for power in the public law. The law which was hammered out by class struggle was called the *ius civile*, civil law. Most nations have a ready-made law from the beginning, a facade law, one to which no reality need correspond. In Rome this class struggle dominated the whole process of devolution until its legal aspect was settled, about 287, when the plebiscite became binding on the entire nation. A knowledge of the laws passed during this period provides an accurate historical sequence of the devolution of the common will.

The second phase of Roman law begins to develop after 287. It starts with the Punic Wars when the Romans set up a "Monroe Doctrine." The peninsula of Italy now belongs to Rome, and she negotiates no terms of surrender or peace with her enemies as long as they stand on Italian soil. If they want to negotiate peace, they must leave Italy.

The kind of law which developed during the second phase is called *ius gentium*, the law of nations. This was the law which the Romans developed after they had become one-willed, which defined the manner in which they would deal with other nations who were also one-willed. The *ius gentium* included several varieties of relations of Rome to her neighbors, allies and foreigners. There were laws for friendly neighbors, there were laws for trade and there were laws for war and for the peoples that were conquered in war. These laws culminate in 146, when Rome had mastered the Mediterranean world.

The third phase of Roman law, the *ius naturale*, was an effort to digest the laws developed during the preceding phases, after the principle that had made these laws possible, the external enemy, was removed.

When Rome was left without an external enemy, she had to develop some way of keeping her laws from ceasing to function. At first there was a period of about 100 years of bitter civil wars. Rome would not have been able to salvage her laws, had it not been that she assimilated the thinking of one of her conquered peoples, the Greeks.

Before she applied Greek reason to her law of nations, the entire edifice had almost toppled. The synthesis of the laws, the combination of all the stages of their development to the Roman law which becomes rational, is called natural law. It is the law of Rome until it fails to work and is finally laid in its tomb in 526.

Roman law, then, consists of three phases. The first phase is the result of class struggle. The second is the result of trade and war, and the third is the result of the application of reason.

To understand Roman history, it is necessary to always keep its laws clearly fixed in the memory. For it is these laws, not philosophy as with the Greeks, that makes the Romans meaningful.

By 287 B.C. Rome arrived at a stage where the conflict between the aristocrats and the plebeians was settled.[17] A new conflict now emerged. Rome was in a pregnant position. A decision had to be made.[18] Rome had reached a moment comparable to the moment the United States has reached today.

It was a moment where great men began to get great perspectives. We too are beginning to get perspectives. The United States has passed out of the stage of *economia*, household management; it has piled up its common wealth to a point where more effective ways of improving the commonwealth suggest themselves. When a nation, in its phase of *economia*, has its house well managed, its best talents are left free to think of other things. It then becomes political. It is a time for everybody to have a share in the common well being. When a nation makes up its mind, it passes out of *economia* into *politeia*. This was the moment Rome had reached in 287.

Polybius regards the assistance given to the Mamartines as the beginning of his history. The decision the Romans had to make was tremendous. It was not customary for the Romans to come to the assistance of other peoples. The question was debated in the Senate. Who are these Mamartines? Are they not renegade Samnites who have been our enemies all along? The Mamartines were using a Castro technique. Castro did not solicit the aid of Russia without at the same time asking the United States for aid. The Mamartines had appealed for help to Carthage, but also to Rome. And both Carthage and Rome decided to help the poor Mamartines in their struggle against Greek Syracuse. In fact, they fought each other in order to help them. (The greatest cause of World War III will be the fight to help the underprivileged areas.) Eduard Meyer says of this moment that Rome and Carthage were destined to conflict. They had a compact not to intervene with each other's affairs. Each feared the other's sphere of influence. When in 264 the Mamartines appealed to both of them for aid against Hiero of Syracuse, Rome was not untroubled by moral scruples, nor was she blind to the fact that to help the Mamartines would lead to war. But the opportunity was too tempting. If she did not intervene, Sicily would fall to Carthage, who was already very strong. The senators hesitated but the Consul Appius Claudius forced the decision. The decision led to an irreversible series of consequences. The immediate consequence was the twenty-four year struggle for Sicily. The ultimate consequence was a realm beyond the sea ruled by Italian magnates. This was the moment that also precipitated the transformation of Rome from the role of a debtor nation, dependent on the imports of goods from other nations, a victim of an unfavorable balance of trade, to that of a creditor nation. *When a nation becomes a creditor, it is transformed not only in its external relations, but it is transformed internally as well.* (This also has happened to the United States.)

During the course of the Punic Wars, which followed the decision to aid the Mamartines, there was great suffering and grief. But there was also prosperity, and no grief was suffered that money could not later wipe out. Even the citizens on the losing side, like maggots on a dead horse, found that in defeat their private life could be facilitated. For the victor, life was heightened to a new level.

Roman history is a history of compromise among interests. A true compromise of interests in order to be achieved must rest on two real interests. The patricians had greedy interests but so had the plebeians. When both of these interests conflicted, as they frequently did, it was possible to arrange a compromise only on the basis of a solid common greed.

During the period of compromises, the early stage of the Roman Republic, the common greed might have been sated by taking the surplus from the minority and distributing it among the majority, giving everyone thereby an equal share in the commonwealth. The fallacy of this approach would have been that the confiscation of the goods of the minority, the aristocracy, would have left that talented segment of the state discontent and it was needed to hold the state together. What was to prevent some external enemy from intervening, should such a confiscation have been attempted, and giving the Romans a genuinely equal share in the commonwealth by removing it altogether; that is to say, giving them all equal shares in nothing? Instead of taking from one of its classes to placate another of its classes, was there not a superior way of making the Romans happy? What if a way was found not of redistributing the common wealth, but of increasing it to such an extent that even the lowest classes would gain more materially than they would have gained through the confiscation of the goods of the aristocracy? How was this to be done? By helping the Mamartines!

During the long period of compromises between patricians and plebeians, genuine concessions were granted the plebs, but this process had to stop short of the annihilation of the aristocracy.

Of this period, the first period in Roman History, Hegel says:

> . . . the plebs attained the right of being eligible to the higher political offices, and that by a share which they too managed to obtain in the land and soil, the means of subsistence were assured to the citizens. By this union of the patriciate and the plebs, Rome first attained true internal consistency, and only after this had been realized could the Roman power develop itself externally. A period of satisfied absorption in the common interest ensues, and the citizens are weary of internal struggles. When after civil discords nations direct their energies outward, they appear in their greatest strength; for the previous excitement continues, and, no longer having its object within, seeks for it without. This direction given to the Roman energies was able for a moment to conceal the defect of that union; equilibrium was restored, but without an essential center of unity and support. The contradiction that existed could not but break out again fearfully at a later period; but previously to this time the greatness of Rome had to display itself in war and the conquest of the world. The power, the wealth, the glory derived from these wars, as also the difficulties to which they led, kept the Romans together as regards the internal affairs of the State. (*Philosophy of History*, 303-304)

In his *Philosophy of Right* Hegel looks at the problem of poverty in a state, and up to a point he was read very carefully by Marx. In essence he observes that not only caprice, but physical contingencies reduce men to poverty. When a society withdraws the natural means of acquisition from its members, as when the farmer is forced to abandon his native soil and is driven to the city, it leaves men in a position of being unable to practice the skills which they know best. The city is paved with stone; there is no place where a farmer can grow his crops. Having been uprooted from his soil, the farmer is also uprooted from his natural family ties. In a condition of poverty he is not only deprived of his skills, but also of the possibility of an education by which he might have acquired new skills. He is deprived of justice.

In this situation, the public authority, the state, has to take the place of the family. It has to try to determine the causes of penury and to attempt to develop procedures to cope with them. But the problem of poverty does not arise only with the displaced farmer. It is implicit in the society which is in a state of unimpeded material activity engaged in internal expansion. The needs of men in such a society will be linked very closely to each other. This will tend to produce a growing division of labor. Men will be forced to specialize. But high specialization degrades a man. It makes him useless when his specialty becomes obsolete. When, as a result of this, the standard of living drops below what is minimally appropriate to the citizen, creation of a rabble of paupers is inevitable. Hegel, in this analysis, was thinking not about England, but about Rome. Now, when the masses have declined to poverty, the burden of this might be placed on the upper classes. But receiving aid directly violates the self respect of the receiver as well as of the giver. So it is apparent that although a society may enjoy great wealth, large sections of it may be poverty stricken. Marx followed Hegel up to this point, but it was not until Lenin that the rest of Hegel's analysis was taken seriously. Hegel went on to observe that *there is an inner dialectic in a civil society which forces it to push outward beyond its own limits in order to achieve a stability within its own limits*. It seeks other markets for its goods. If necessary, it creates other markets in the backward areas of the world. This is precisely what the Romans did.

But in doing this, something else happened to the

Romans.

The outcome of the First Punic War had not been a real victory. Rome met the great test in the Second Punic War when Hannibal defeated her at Cannae. The Second Punic War produced a modern leader in Fabius Cunctator, "The Delayer." What is modern about Fabius? We have a society named after him. The tactics of the Fabian society are identical with those of the Roman prototype. Its motto is, "Do not meet the capitalists head on, but follow them around." Fabius the Delayer's policy was not popular among the Romans. How was the unbeatable Hannibal to be beaten?

How does the Fabian Society propose to beat the free enterprise system? Fabius said Hannibal can be beaten by not being directly attacked. The policy of Fabius impaired the power of Hannibal without hitting him directly.

The heroic Romans learned a lesson only after they rashly struck at Hannibal and suffered their disastrous defeat at Cannae (216). It was after Cannae that the Romans realized that, although all the offices of state were open to the plebs, not all the plebs could fill these offices. They began to look around for people who knew how to get things done. It was essential to learn whom to listen to and whom not to listen to.

If something must get done, it is possible to call upon a man fresh out of Harvard. But if it really must get done, then perhaps it is wiser not to call upon a man who will give elaborate psychological reasons for hating the enemy, and instead put in power a man like Franklin Delano Roosevelt, who only wanted to beat Germany very badly because he could not accept the idea of losing.

The impulsive Roman general, Varro, survived the catastrophe at Cannae. Polybius reserves for him his most biting criticism, that it was difficult to beat Hannibal because it was necessary to fight two generals, Hannibal and Varro. Varro impressed on the people the truth that a man who talks big does not always do big things. So the people turned to the fathers, the patrician families who took over and planned the campaign. They moved assuming magistracies out of the Senate and began to dominate. They truly divested themselves of their wealth for the sake of Rome. They were not, as so often happens when an enterprise appears lost, eager to flee like birds before an earthquake. They won the war.

Hannibal, before the final battle at Zama (202), asked the Carthaginians to remember the battles of Trebia at the Trasimene Lake and Cannae, and to remember that the men they were about to face were either children of those men they had slaughtered or derelicts from those wars. Scipio, who had no reason to believe he could beat Hannibal, and who would never have been able to beat him had Hannibal not been forced to use mercenaries, also spoke to the Romans before the battle. He urged them to think what victory would mean. They would be masters of Africa. But if conquered, they would have gloriously died for their country. "Retain not thought of life," he said. The sentiments of Scipio have since been expressed again and again at Agincourt, by Frederick the Great, at Stalingrad. Let us meet in victory or never meet again. These sentiments of war belong to rhetoric.

Scipio admired Hannibal. Soldiers have a great deal in common, but then so do the enemies of soldiers.

Polybius observes that the Rome of his time was Rome in her heyday. She had achieved her peak. Her chief antagonist, Carthage, had passed her peak. This largely accounts for the fact that Rome triumphed over Carthage. In Carthage, Polybius points out, there was popular rule. The term popular rule, as employed by all Greek political analysts, means the rule of those who produce.

In Carthage it was the people, that is to say, capital and labor, who were in charge. They controlled Hannibal, whose only ambition from childhood on had been to fight Rome. In Rome, Polybius observes, there were aristocrats who were still behaving like aristocrats. Carthage was at a time when the worker-group was determining everything.

Carthage was truly a city-state. She never developed the ability to integrate with her allies. She knew that if she shared her prosperity with her allies, she would surrender her gains. It is difficult to maintain the standard of living and good will of one's own people without sacrificing the friendship of other peoples. Carthage's allies were resentful. But the allies alone were not treated as mercenaries. Hannibal himself was in a sense a mercenary, looked down upon by Carthaginian statesmen. He had to develop his own source of supply in Spain.

Carthage had been at her best before the Punic Wars. At Zama she had already declined. Her aristocracy completely failed to fulfill its function. The function of an aristocracy is to fight.

The end of the war was a triumph for the Roman aristocrats, but also for everyone else. There was a re-alignment of classes. The marvel of the Roman constitution was such that the upper bourgeoisie was immediately admitted into the class of patricians. (It took Britain many years to grudgingly accomplish the same thing.) But just as quickly, there was a new class struggle. The plebs had gotten every single thing that they had asked for. It is very difficult when progress reaches such a point that no one will consent to clean up the normal filth of a city. There are countries today, like Italy, where no one will clean up except perhaps an old man who has lost his spirit of freedom.

After these bitterly fought-over victories, Rome started reaching out for plums. What did the Romans want with the East? Perhaps in the spirit of our Peace Corps, they went there to help the helpless help themselves. The man who does this feels like a king because he has come to help. But it is hard to keep a religious zeal when there is nothing left to fight about. After the Romans liberated Greece, what was there left to do? They could keep the books of the provinces. They could keep a record of the taxes they collected, if they were able to collect the taxes. But what was the point of collecting the taxes? Whom should they be sent to? Why send them anywhere? After all, there were the collectors, and the governor of the province, and there always has been wine, women, and song. How about a villa with an ocean under it?

Rome had already experimented with the welfare state. Everybody had the only thing that was left to pursue, happiness. Everything was settled. Everybody had everything. Everybody was happy. But when everybody has everything, somebody will always have more of everything than somebody else. And since everybody has everything, everybody has eloquence. Before not too long there will be eloquent complaints about that somebody who has more of everything. It is more painful to be discriminated against in happiness than in food.

In the interval between the Second and Third Punic Wars, the appetites of the Romans were being whetted with material vices. The Roman indulged himself in delicacies and fancy eating, in deliberate excesses which were calculated to impress everyone with opulence, like the well-to-do man who makes it a point to have more food at his party than he can possibly use, and as he throws away the surplus, makes scrupulously certain that everyone sees him throwing it away.

Among the spoils of the Second Punic War were the means to satisfy the newly acquired Roman appetite for luxury and entertainment: the plays of Plautus (Jack Paar, Jack Benny, and script-writers — Rome had them all). The returning Roman warriors were in no way different from our own farm boys coming back from Europe. "How are you goin' to keep 'em down on the farm after they've seen Paree?" They brought back famous Greek celebrations, the Bacchanals. The pagans were notorious for the festivals they celebrated.

Among the spoils was the practice of tax-farming,

which made many people very rich. The tax farmer resembles the professional fund raiser of our own day, who has mastered the difficult art of extracting maximum contributions from unwilling donors. This had been simplified for the Roman tax farmer by the oriental peoples themselves whose government had long ago developed this art to perfection. All the Romans had to do was step in and take over the elaborate machinery of tax collection which they had inherited. Another part of the spoils were the slaves. These were the people who did the menial work that was beneath the Roman citizen — the dishwashers of Rome.

The tax farmers became very generous; some of their revenue found its way into the Latin versions of the Ford Foundations and Rockefeller Institutes.

Rome had inherited a taste for luxury from the East and from the Greeks. She probably could have coped with the luxury, but she inherited something else from Greece which was more deadly—the intelligence of Greece.

What came rushing into Rome at this point? Was it the greatness of Ancient Greece? Was it the intelligence of Hellenic Greece? Quite the contrary, it was defeated Greece. It was to this that Rome was exposed.

There was a time when the Greek spoke about a state that would combine the virtues of Sparta and Athens. But that was an earlier Greece. The Greece of Cato's day had turned away from this and searched for happiness in herself.

What captivated the Roman mind? The three big sects of ancient Greece which had absorbed the earlier institutions of Greek thinking: skepticism, epicureanism, stoicism.

The Academy of Plato was now infiltrated with skeptics. The school of Plato, the man who had been the great antagonist of skeptics, had become skeptical. The skeptic would agree that Plato was a great thinker, but he had insisted on adequate ideas, and who is there to judge

what ideas are adequate? If the skeptic was reminded that
doubt is only the beginning of wisdom, that the ladder of
knowledge can never be climbed with one foot on the
ground, he would reply that this may have been so before.
But now there is no state, and the only place where
intellectual life can flourish is in the mind of the solitary
thinker. This Greek mentality was scattered over the Mediterranean, and it took possession of the higher Roman.

There was epicureanism. The entertainment came
first; the doctrine came later. Epicurus may have found his
highest pleasure in abstract thought, but it was still pleasure that he was concerned with. What pleases one man
need not necessarily please another. Every man was free to
find his own highest pleasure.

The social contract theory is epicurean. The epicurean reasoned that the worst state of being would be to
never enjoy any pleasure at all. In order to forestall the
possibility of enjoying no pleasure at all, even though his
primary aim was to enjoy all the pleasure he could, the
epicurean agreed not to push his pursuit of pleasure to
such an extent that it would conflict with anyone else's
pursuit of pleasure, provided that everyone else would also
restrain his pursuit of pleasure. In this way, everyone could
enjoy some pleasure without anyone being forced to enjoy
no pleasure at all.

Rome was to pass a law against epicurianism, but
the upper class of Romans, among whom were the Gracchi,
influenced by the tutelage of men like Polybius, were
captivated by the stoic mentality. They adopted the mentality of the stoic, not his philosophy.

Stoic philosophy is the emptiest the world has ever
known. The stoic ethic, however, struck a responsive chord
in the Romans. The stoic motto, in effect, was that one does
right because one must do it. It is one's painful duty. This
culminated in the height of moral snobbery. Men began to
act so much like gods that they thought they were gods.
Little wonder that the stoic ethics were opposed by both

Christianity and Judaism. The stoic classification of people was that they were good, bad and indifferent. Though they were not worthy of it, the stoic would love them all. This doctrine of ethics was typified by Tiberius Gracchus, who was so far above everybody that even Cato and Scipio appeared like nobodies by comparison. This way of thinking was the first "be kind to animals" mentality. It gave rise to humanitarians who wanted to include everyone in the benevolent sweep of their justice. It pushed Roman law into a broader and broader scope until it came to include the enemy as well as the Romans. This process culminated in Natural Law which included all humanity. The only way that it could have gone beyond this would have been to include all animals as well.

The best vices of Greece were reserved for the higher classes and it was stoicism of which the Greeks were most proud. The stoic became the master of the master of Rome. Stoicism was among the spoils of war. The chief vehicle of stoicism as it came into the Roman republic was the Greek, Panaetius.

When stoicism brought justice to Rome, what happened?

If justice were brought to a band of thieves, what would happen? They would get punished. Justice will put the Romans into jail, where they properly belong, but they will call their prison by other names.

The old post-Alexandrian stoicism had been a dogmatic school of thought. It was dogmatic because it accepted principles which it knew led to an irreconcilable contradiction. In this respect it resembled the dilemma that the Catholic Church was later to face, in accepting as true two principles which can never be reconciled by reason: that on the one hand, God is omnipotent and that on the other, man is free. When Luther claimed he could prove that man was not free, the only answer the church could give was that to the Catholics man is free because they accept his freedom on faith. This is the kind of dogmatism the old stoicism was grounded in.

The old stoicism emerged from the disintegration of Hellenic Greek society. Hellenic philosophy, as opposed to the old stoic, had held that the state was a necessary means for attaining knowledge. It held that the state should be a combination of reason and power personified in the philosopher-king. It was the nature of man to desire happiness and knowledge, and he had to form a state which would enable him to realize these ends.

In such a state, the Hellenic philosophers Plato and Aristotle contended, happiness would be realized by everyone in different ways. The highest happiness would belong to the guardian of the state, the philosopher-king, who would find it in knowledge. The next highest happiness would be that of the soldier, the protector of the state, who would find it in honor. The lowest form of happiness would be enjoyed by the producers of the state, in pleasure. But how are these three varieties of happiness to be pursued when there is no state?

The post-Alexandrian thinker fragmented them.

But Aristotle and Plato held they could not be fragmented. They said that in order to enjoy any of them they all had to be present. There would be no knowledge, or honor, or pleasure separately, but only in the organic totality of a state in which a guiding, fighting, and producing class interacted.

But what was to be done when there existed no such state? The post-Alexandrian's reply was, that which was to be done must be done by the individual alone.

An individual alone, removed from the setting of a city-state, was obligated to whom? To everybody. Everybody was his brother. This was a much bigger obligation than being a citizen of Athens, or of the Persian Empire. He was the citizen of Mankind.

This proved to be a much easier burden to bear. Has anyone ever paid taxes to mankind or served in the army of mankind? By being obligated to everybody, the post-Alexandrian was in actuality obligated to nobody.

To the solitary individual, what did knowledge mean? The skeptic made knowledge an eternal quest. Truth is always beyond the grasp of the intellect. He was in an endless pursuit of it, knowing there was no chance of catching it.

If any of these three Greek sects had stopped at some principle, a government would have been formed around it. Had they named a truth, it would have been the nucleus for a city-state. But this was done in earlier years in the Greece of the Hellenic period, and now in post-Alexandrian times there was no state. What is to be done when there is no state?

The stoic and the epicurean said that since no one any longer has the truth, let us be still. Why was the stoic empty? What specific duty did he have? Stoicism said the life of honor was always worth living, and if it became too unbearable, one could always die. Stoicism advised man to rip out his passions. Contrary to Aristotle, who had held that the passions should be trained, to the stoic, life was highest without passion.

The old stoic, then, developed the doctrine which had been familiar to the Greeks, of the strong individual man.

Panaetius, who was the teacher of the teacher of Cicero, gave stoicism a new twist that made it acceptable to Rome. The concept of strong individuals was alien to the Romans; they tended rather to think in terms of the class.

At this time in Rome's history, a new class was emerging between the rich and the poor, the haves and have-nots. Whenever there is dissension between two classes, the usual remedy is an intermediary force, the half-rich and half-poor, the middle class. The middle class is always a stabilizing influence.

The natural drive of the upper class is to devour the lower class; whereas the natural drive of the lower class is to divide the wealth of the upper class among its members.

They both represent absolutisms in the state.

The function of the middle class is to mechanically stabilize these extremities — because its interests are bound up in both classes. But what if in place of this mechanical intervention, there was substituted another stabilizer, a kind of Solon, a mediator without interest, in a word, justice?

There were the very rich, the Roman capitalists, and the discontented poor, who were not so poor, and in between was the middle class. The middle class was the land-owning aristocracy that was not capitalistic and did not know that it was the middle class because of prestige from family aristocrats. It was too sophisticated to serve a mechanical function in the state. It had prestige; it was literate. It listened to the Greeks who talked about justice. Its members were the first to hear about justice.

Among its members was Scipio (Africanus) who opposed the destruction of Carthage, believing that it should be kept as a kind of club over the heads of the quarreling factions that might otherwise be reluctant to reason out their differences. Through Scipio this new stoicism entered Rome.

The concept of the great man, the individual, had been characteristic of the Greeks since Thales. But the Romans thought in terms of classes, not great men. It occurred to Panaetius that stoicism might be modified from its old status of a philosophy for individuals to a philosophy for a class.

We know about Panaetius from Cicero. No writing of Panaetius has survived. He held that the best men should direct their energies to the public welfare. The best men were those who had habitual mastery of their appetites, something which the old Romans had prided themselves on. They called it gravitas, the heaviness of duty. Furthermore, these energies were to be directed not toward the old stoic mankind but to the state. And the wise man of old stoic philosophy now blended with the statesman.

The Romans were the only people who could reconcile the somberness of stoicism with a state.

Scipio Nasica echoed this teaching with the conviction that the wise man was in no sense a private man. Cato, who admired the Greek thinking, feared the effects its individualism would have on Roman solidarity.

Panaetius and Polybius gave the Romans a philosophy that was not individualistic, a class philosophy.

The class had to be wise. The state had to be governed by the class. If an individual tried to administer justice, according to Panaetius, Polybius and Scipio, there would be a monarchy.

This is the purpose for which Polybius wrote his histories: to educate statesmen. He wrote about what had actually happened, but he wrote also about what he thought had happened and would happen. And his message very plainly to the Roman statesmen was to use their restraining force.

Rome came to be conquered by Greece, through the friendship of a Greek political scientist, Polybius, and a Roman general, Scipio.

Polybius had gotten to know Scipio by sending a few books to his parents. His intimacy with Scipio grew. Later, when the Acheaen hostages with whom Polybius was brought to Rome were being distributed to various Italian cities, Scipio arranged to have Polybius remain in Rome. Under Polybius' influence, Scipio developed into a remarkably liberal man; to the point of making unprofitable financial gestures to his relatives, something which a Roman never did.

It had always been characteristic of the Romans that each man was concerned with his own interests and if he needed something the other would not give, he would pull a strike. But Scipio was actually thinking in terms of interests other than his own. He became attached to the sophistication of Greece and yet retained the essential Roman virtues. He was a combination of qualities which one would expect to find in Adlai Stevenson and a hardened warrior; a combination of Greek civilization and Roman power.

The Roman legal approach to other nations involved knowing, first of all, exactly what the laws of those nations were. The Romans listed the laws of the nations they conquered. Before a Roman governor pronounced an edict, he examined lists of extant laws of his province to see if any corresponded to his edict. This approach made his edict frequently appear not as an edict at all but as an expression of the conquered peoples' own laws.

It would be unwise for a conqueror nation to simply tear down the laws of a defeated nation before examining them, as this indiscriminate pulling down of all existing local laws would make the conqueror appear as an oppressor. Whereas by a nullification of a few of the less useful native laws, the conqueror would appear to the conquered as a tolerant liberator.

Fascist laws are more severe than American laws. Would it not be foolish to try to displace Fascist laws with American laws in a conquered Fascist nation, when the Americans would gain the gratitude of the conquered peoples and earn the appearance of being genuine benefactors, merely by abolishing those laws which the conquered peoples themselves despised while retaining those laws which would provide the desired results far more efficiently than substitute American laws?

The Romans also listed the laws governing trade of different nations. America tried the other approach and it proved unsuccessful. She would trade with other nations only on her own terms. This led to wide commercial resistance. The Romans learned the commercial procedures of their conquered peoples and carried on transactions with these peoples insofar as possible within these procedures. If a Roman were dealing with a non-Roman, he realized he could not deal with him as if he were a

Roman. The Roman kept as much of the non-Roman's law as he needed, alongside his own Roman laws. In the course of such transactions, a scheme of laws began to emerge. The Roman examined the lists of laws of other nations and weeded out those which were too local, keeping those which appeared to be common to all the nations. This body of laws was the *ius gentium*.

The Romans kept their own civil laws, *ius civile*. But along with these they developed *ius gentium,* which included those civil laws all nations had or would have wanted to have. The *ius civile* was the civil law of Rome and the *ius gentium* was a composite of the civil laws of nations outside of Rome.

Roman civil law had developed over the years through social crises; it was only through a long class strife that the Romans acquired *ius civile*. The *ius gentium*, which the Romans formulated, was able to do for a conquered nation, immediately and without the usual class strife, what it took Rome many years to do for herself. Roman law was a great liberation for the non-Roman.

When Panaetius and Polybius came to Rome and saw the *ius gentium* which was forming, they noted it was very similar to the law that the Greeks had been thinking about since Greece fell. A real law, however, is never obtained by thinking alone. It is the result of a compromise of interests. A compromise of interests can arise only within a state. The Greeks, since they had no state, could not use compromise as a basis for formulating a law. Their law came from reason. It was called natural law. Like their philosophy, it was conceived to be universal. This Greek approach to law influenced the Romans. Between the first century B.C. and the first century A.D., the Romans assimilated it into their legal thinking. It was ultimately given precise formulation in the *Index* of Justinian. In it the Romans distinguished the laws under which every community was governed. These laws were partly those of the community, *ius civile*, civil law, and partly those common to all communities, *ius gentium*, law of nations. But *ius naturale*, the law of natural reason, appointed the law for all mankind.

The Roman saw the tragedy implied in *ius civile* and *ius gentium*, for they arose out of the necessity in human life to compromise. And the saddest observation ever made was that out of disparities among nations as expressed in the law of nations, wars arose and in their train followed captivity. When a stronger nation conquers a weaker nation and offers terms of unconditional surrender, the conquered nation is truly in a state of captivity.

To the Roman, captivity meant slavery and slavery meant despair.[19] To the Hellenized Roman, slavery was contrary to the law of nature as formulated by reason. By that law all men were born free.

The Roman defined what freedom was. Freedom as applied to man was the natural power to do as he pleases, unless he is prevented to do so by force and by law.[20]

The Roman concluded that slavery comes from the law of nations. Slaves are either born by their slave mothers or become slaves through captivity. Just as the slave existed because of his definition in the law of nations, so did the freedman exist because he was freed from the laws of slavery. The freedman, too, was a result of the law of nations.

But by the law of nature, the Hellenized Roman reminds us that all men were born free. Under the law of nature, everyone was free, but because of the law of nations three classes of men emerged: freemen, slaves, and freedmen.[21]

Cato was a realistic man. He saw that Rome's expansion had weakened the fiber of the Romans. There was something evil in everybody being a college graduate and having two Cadillacs in the garage. When a country starts importing caviar from the Black Sea, it is time to be careful. At Zama Rome had had men. But now everyone was a

Harvard graduate. Cato had two suggestions. First of all, stop this corruption of Romans. But there was not much that could be done about corruption. Secondly, Carthage must be destroyed. He ended all his speeches with this phrase.

There was another man in Rome, Scipio Nasica, who ended all his speeches differently: Carthage must not be destroyed.

Cato was a man who wanted the aristocrats not to lose their disposition to fight. Cato was a Roman of the antique stance. He may be regarded as an opponent of the Hellenic stance. The aristocrats of his day were coming back to Rome from faraway lands with dangerous ideas. They were critical of the industrious lower middle class. They had not thought of working for fifteen generations, but they had something more noble. They had justice.

Cato feared that Rome could not beat a new enemy, if the enemy was allowed to grow strong,

Cato, the man who called for the destruction of Carthage, came from the ranks of the people. He was concerned about raising the standard of living of the masses, far more so than was Scipio. Cato represented that movement which was concerned with the devolution of power. He wanted to pull the power down from the aristocrats but, like a good Englishman, not all the way. He knew that if it was pulled down entirely to his level, it would quickly slip out of his control to the masses below. Scipio Nasica, on the other hand, represented the restraining group.[22] He disapproved of his relative, Gaius Gracchus. To him, the balance of power in the state could only be kept if it had a powerful enemy, an external enemy.

Plutarch cites the controversy between Cato and Scipio over Carthage. He says:

> Moreover, they say that, shaking his gown, he [Cato] took occasion to let drop some African figs before the senate. And on their admiring the size and beauty of them, he presently added that the place that bore them

was but three days sail from Rome. Nay, he never after gave his opinion. but at the end he would be sure to come out with this sentence: "Also, Carthage, methinks, ought utterly to be destroyed." But Publius Scipio Nasica would always declare his opinion to the contrary, in these words, "It seems requisite to me that Carthage should still stand." For seeing his countrymen to be grown wanton and insolent, and the people made, by their prosperity, obstinate and disobedient to the senate, and drowning the whole city, whither they would, after them, he would have had the fear of Carthage to serve as a bit to hold the contumacy of the multitude; and he looked upon the Carthaginians as too weak to overcome the Romans, and too great to be despised by them.

Cato became famous as a censor in the modern sense. He concentrated on censoring the Roman swells. He concentrated on the people who were indulging themselves most conspicuously. These were the big people in Roman society. And it was because they were the big people that their excesses were the most dangerous. He did not mean to imply that the people of the lower classes were good and those of the upper classes were bad. He rather intended to make examples of the upper classes to the lower, showing them their own vices magnified.

Where were the heroes of earlier time?

Let us start a third Punic War, Cato demanded, and create some heroes. A third Punic war would raise the standard of living of Rome's lower class, and by destroying Rome's only competitor, remove the necessity of worrying about a favorable balance of trade.

III. THE SECOND PHASE

THE FALL OF THE REPUBLIC FROM THE DESTRUCTION OF CARTHAGE IN *146 B.C.* TO THE DEATH OF AUGUSTUS IN *14 A.D.*

The provocation for the destruction of Carthage was the desire for an increased standard of living. Cato's policy prevailed. *The Roman Republic is the only example in history of what happens to a nation that has no external enemy.*

In the presence of an external enemy, it was very easy to have the people put aside their differences. It became far more difficult in time of peace. When there was an enemy, the hatred that the lower class had for the upper class could be poured on the enemy. We have seen this in our own history when the country was divided against itself over whether aid should be sent to Britain in her struggle against Germany. All this was swept away with the Japanese attack on Pearl Harbor. When a common enemy appears, a voice like that of Scipio or FDR is heard.

After the destruction of Carthage, Roman history was studded with many wars. But these were not real wars against formidable enemies who had a chance of beating Rome. They were all propaganda wars that had to be made to appear dangerous, just as in time of peace we invent numerous wars, wars on crime, wars on sickness.

After the destruction of Carthage, a hundred Catos descended on the political scene. The best technique for a man to succeed in politics is either to become a censor, bringing to the attention of the people those men of the opposite faction who have abused the public trust, or to become a political martyr. How many political careers have been launched when the popular leader is carried away to jail from the scene of some calculated mob protest?

What is done about quarreling factions when a real peace is achieved and there is no possibility of inventing a war? Reason is appealed to. But reason is buried the instant a man cries faction.

St. Augustine, who had given considerable thought to it, was asked to explain the fall of Rome. Why had it come to pass that Rome in 410 A.D. was sacked by barbarians for the first time in 800 years? The usual explanation was rooted in pre-Augustinian Roman thinking, the explanation later to be used by Gibbon, that Christianity had led to the loss of the manly virtues; that the people of Rome because they had a Christian Emperor had lost the will to fight.

St. Augustine wrote *The City of God* to answer this line of thinking. He contended that the Romans were prone to condemn Christianity, not because it restrained them from defending the state, but because they would rather not be criticized for their vices. He cites the controversy over Carthage where Scipio, the best man from among the Romans, would not have Carthage subverted and contradicted Cato, pointing out that Carthage was a necessary tutor and terror.

St. Augustine says that when Carthage had been brought to nothing, Rome was subjected to many inconveniences, to civil wars, to slaughter, to too much inhumanity. The destruction of Carthage, according to St. Augustine, was the beginning of Rome's long decline.

Many things have been said about the fall of the Republic as well as the fall of the Empire, but the fall of the Empire was merely a five hundred year delay in the ultimate collapse of the Republic.

A delicate balance was maintained for about ten years after the third Punic War, and then havoc reigned.

When finally the Romans failed in their effort to make an entire class the best, individuals began to step forward in the name of justice. Tiberius Gracchus would be the first, and Caesar would be the last.

The correction of the *ius civile* and *ius gentium* by reason is the background for the activities of the Gracchi and their successors. Personalities such as Marius, Sulla, Caesar, hammered the law of reason into Roman law, which resisted reason. The Greek concept of justice was destined to disrupt Roman society; it had to be impressed on it by force. Justice was one of the spoils of the Punic Wars.

When justice finally came in, woe to the pirates of Romulus. What happens when there is no external enemy? As long as there is an enemy and there is war or the threat of war, men are free. But when there is no enemy and the peace has been won, men lose their freedom.

The Roman Republic was ruined by justice. The stoics retained the pure doctrine of the Greek world, which the Romans were to instinctively make their own. The stoic preached: "to each his due," and this is what is going to cause all the trouble.

The concept enters the Roman world and was to be expressed by Tiberius Gracchus, who came from one of the most prominent families in Rome and was the nephew of the greatest Roman, Scipio Africanus.

The Roman mob which elected him to the tribunate in 133 B.C., and in whose name he was to speak, was described by Mommsen thus:

> . . . the populace was also a great lord, and desired its share of attention. The rabble began to demand as its right that the future consul should recognize and honor the sovereign people in every ragged idler of the street, and that every candidate should in his "going round," salute every individual voter by name and press his hand. The world of quality readily entered into this degrading canvas. The candidate cringed not only in the palace but also on the street, and recommended himself to the multitude by flattering attentions, indulgences, and ci-

vilities. (*History of Rome*, 23)

The candidates who willingly submitted to these indignities were usually millionaires (Harriman, Kennedy and Rockefeller have "gone round"). Tiberius Gracchus, speaking of the same mob, said:

> The wild beasts that roam Italy. . . have their dens and lairs to shelter them, but the men who fight and die for Italy have nothing but air and light. Homeless and footless, they wander about with their wives and children. In battle their generals exhort them to defend their sepulchers and shrines from the enemy; they lie. Not one among the host of Romans has his ancestral altar or the tomb of his fathers; it is for the wealth and luxury of others that they fight and die. They are called masters of the world, they have no clod of earth to call their own.

Had Tiberius Gracchus said this in 509 B.C. instead of 133 B.C., it would have been true. But this kind of a speech can only be delivered to a people who have achieved some prosperity and are in a position to want more. Were things really better in the past, as Tiberius claimed? Were they better at the battle of Cannae?

The Rome of Tiberius Gracchus was just like the world of today where surplus capital is available and freely dispensed. It had its grants and foundations and statesmen traveling to far away places sponsored by charitable organizations.

When the Italians closed their country villas and brought their families to the city to find they could not get in on that surplus capital, Tiberius said of them, "homeless and footless, they wander about with their wives and children."

There were other problems Tiberius Gracchus had to face. Rome did not need the small farmer. The attempt to restore him is comparable to Ghandi's attempt to restore hand-weaving. How could the small farmer compete with the big farms which were operated by cheap labor, talented slaves who could till the soil better, keep the books better, and maintain a higher level of efficiency? It was true that the Latifundia was more efficient and made more money than small farming could, but there were some things that money could not buy. Money cannot buy morale, self-confidence and dignity, nor can it efface the lack of these.

The small farmer had been the respected head of a family. He had had the dignity that the head of a household can enjoy on the farm, but not in a city apartment. The family might not be too important if one lived under the ideally functioning republic of Plato, but it becomes profoundly important when the state is purposeless; even Plato, in his later years, was to point this out.

Tiberius Gracchus was a sophisticated, intelligent man with a noble heart. A noble heart does more evil than anything else. And as the heart gets more and more noble, the violence gets more and more brutal. There is never enough might when a man is right.

The mother of Tiberius Gracchus was later to despair that he and his younger brother Gaius had ever been born, proving, perhaps, that class interests run thicker than blood.

Tiberius pondered the situation. What was to be done? The old Roman type was gone. The children did not obey their fathers anymore. This is the way children always behave in the city. The father can never pull rank on his family when they live in an apartment house. He could, it is true, insist on keeping his authority, but he will find that none of his family will stay around to submit to it. He might resort to religion and try to cajole the youngsters to obey father because of the big father up there. If this device works at all, it is only because the big father resembles a farmer so much. One might call this projecting the "farmer image."

Tiberius Gracchus faced the evils created by the Latifundia. The American farm situation has become similarly industrial, only we have industrial farms now, whose magnitude makes the Latifundia seem petty. The proposed solution that Tiberius Gracchus had in mind was seen later by his brother Gaius to be insane .

Many people in Rome actually owned the farms but not the land on which they were situated. The owner of the farm and the owner of the land were two different persons. The land on which Rockefeller Center stands in Manhattan is not owned by the organization that owns the Center. It belongs to Columbia University, which periodically leases it to the Center. This relationship is not so odd. Why should Rockefeller Center own the land on which it stands? Is it likely that Columbia would want to reclaim its land while Rockefeller Center is cluttering it?

So Tiberius proposed to take back some of this land on which the Latifundia stood, and compensate the land-owners for some of their loss. But this aroused tremendous hostility on the part of those who stood to lose in the transaction.

Scipio Aemelianus warned that this proposal was propaganda; the rich class could never believe that it was in its own interests. It carried rather such political advantage for Tiberius that it could not be construed as a politically disinterested proposal. Scipio warned further that if the proposal were forced, it would lead to civil war.

That civil wars have been fought over economic issues has been repeatedly borne out by history. The United States is very familiar with the consequences of a Northern economic interest confronting a Southern economic interest.

Tiberius Gracchus was not afraid of civil war. In our time he is commonly referred to as the F.D.R. of Rome. He has been labeled a tyrant, a tyrant being defined as a benefactor of the people against the other classes. The first famous tyrant of this sort was Pisistratus, in Athens.

Tiberius Gracchus was the first man in Roman history to force a law in an unconstitutional manner by demanding the dismissal of a tribune, thus violating that

inviolable office. He began by calling for the re-instate-
ment of the Licinian Sextian law, but it had a different
value now. This was to be the means for chopping up the
spoils of war lands among the lower classes; the nobles
stood to lose.

Tiberius, a man from a noble family, ran for the
office of tribune and was elected. Another nobleman,
Marcus Octavius, was elected along with Tiberius as tribune.

Tiberius proposed his bill to the lower assembly
and Octavius, upon the instigation of the Senate, vetoed it.
Octavius wanted no part of the bill unless it was supported
by the entire legal machinery of the state. If Tiberius
wanted his bill to pass, he would have to resort to persua-
sion in smoke-filled rooms. The smoke-filled room of
Rome was the Senate.

So Tiberius went to the Senate and stated his case.
He argued that the plebs would become a great danger to
Rome unless they were restored to doing work of some
dignity. The only way to give some spine to the masses was
to get them back on the farm. The Senate accused Tiberius
of being reactionary.

He was in fact being reactionary in wanting to put
people on farms when there was no need for them to be on
farms. The Romans were to get indignant about this. The
very people to whom he wanted to give land were to chop
him down. Tiberius wanted to give them the land to till, but
at the same time remove from them the right to sell the
land to someone else, as any sane city dweller would have
done.

Upon being turned down by the Senate, Tiberius
decided on a new course of action, which was to prove
unconstitutional. He would offer a new bill to the lower
assembly, not this time for the restitution of the Licinian
Sextian law, but a proposal to put to the vote the qualifica-
tions of Octavius to hold office as a tribune of the people.
This proposal was absolutely unconstitutional. Tiberius

took a vote of the lower tribes in the assembly. The issue: was Octavius qualified to hold office?

What Tiberius Gracchus was really questioning was whether the tribune, who for centuries had been inviolate, was really inviolate. He was inaugurating a major constitutional change without resorting to the delicate legal process which constitutional changes require. All Tiberius wanted was a majority vote from the lower classes. If he got this, he felt Octavius could be removed.

The whole transaction might have been legalized had Octavius withdrawn his veto. But Octavius refused. Tiberius got his vote of confidence from the lower classes and Octavius was removed on the grounds that he had lost the faith of the people. But was this a sufficient basis for removing a previously untouchable tribune from office before his term had expired? Octavius reminded Tiberius that the question of whether the tribune had retained the faith of the people was brought up for questioning legally only once a year, when the tribune was running for election. The tribune was not obliged to defend his office every day of his term. Tiberius pushed his illegal vote and had Octavius impeached.

But the notion of impeachment can only be legal when it is operating within the framework of a natural law. Our own concept of impeachment is based on a constitutional definition of what constitutes the correct behavior of an official in office. There was no comparable legal framework in the Roman constitution to justify the action Tiberius was taking.

The office of the tribune had been the first big wedge the lower classes had driven into the otherwise absolute monopoly of government of the upper classes. Tiberius was now violating this. The lower classes were perfectly willing to concede that the aristocracy was the talented segment of Rome, and that it was the aristocracy who was best qualified to run the government. But there would arise times when the aristocracy might use its talents for excessively selfish ends. The institution of the tribune with its negative vote was intended to check this tendency.

How, it might be asked, could the lower classes, most of whom were illiterate, presume to question the decisions of the talented aristocracy? The lower classes may not have been literate and they certainly could have never projected the elaborate plans for government which the aristocracy was expected to provide, but they had their own criteria, irrational as they might have been, with which they evaluated a plan of action proposed by the aristocracy. The farmer might use a criterion as simple as the number of bushels of grain he had to set aside for taxes. The tribune was instituted to express the objection of the constituents to a proposed plan of action. It was really a perfect remedy to the problem. It was a negative remedy. It left the business of formulating the plans to the creative aristocracy, an area in which the lower classes could not compete; but it left the final approval of the plan to the lower classes. If a proposed plan was disliked, the people, through the tribune, could veto it. The people could not plan, but they could adamantly reject a proposed plan and demand the aristocracy wrack its brains to come up with something better. The tribune was supposed to express the will of the people for one year. If Tiberius could have gotten his law through without destroying the tribunate, the aristocracy would probably have eventually constructed a monument to his memory. But he impeached Octavius and, with no further obstacle in his way, he proceeded to look around to see who among the nobility he could trust to institute his reforms. His program was so good for the people that he decided not to take any chances with it and kept it in his family.

The actions of Tiberius had been destroying the real apparatus of government. Was the tribunate as unimportant as Tiberius thought? If one tribune could be impeached when he was seemingly wrong, another could be impeached even if he was right. Where would impeachment stop? If the tribunate was destroyed, the entire fabric of the constitution would be ripped.

The upper class had come to control the tribunate only with great finesse and difficulty. The tribunate had been a fixed feature of the Roman constitution, a tangible instrument for the expression of the will of the people. While the office remained the aristocracy would adjust to it or manipulate it, but if it were removed the will of the people would become imponderable.

The noblemen were disgruntled; Scipio called for another trial. Tiberius had organized a trial made up exclusively of the lower classes. Scipio now got his own class together to vote on the actions of Tiberius. The nobles were by now about as angry at Tiberius as he was at them.

The aristocrats went directly through the crowded streets to get their man, helpfully pointed out by his followers, who did not lift an arm to save their own benefactor from being killed.

Tiberius was not a guilty man; there was a reason for his activity. If he had not done what he did someone else would have, and he was the right man to do it. But Scipio and his peers found him guilty of treason. It was not the people of Rome they condemned, they always did want the lion's share, just as the upper class did. They condemned the man who looked like a demagogue and who began to look like a king. They blamed the aristocratic rabble rouser, Tiberius. No action was to be taken against the people, only against their hero.

It was left to Gaius Gracchus to adapt Tiberius' program to reality. For that, he had to get the support of the people in the city. He could not afford to have a hostile city population against him. But getting this support would be impossible if the cost of foods in the city were to rise with the rise of farm prices. Obviously it was necessary that the prices in the city be cut while the prices on the farm products were permitted to rise. He faced the same problem every liberal administration encounters when it tries to balance the rural interests with the urban interests.

Money was needed to bring about this balance.

Gaius made a brilliant maneuver; he gave tax-farming to the richest people, the nouveaux riches, the equites, not to the nobles. The equites made their fortunes in the East. They had never had much to say about the government because this had remained in the hands of the nobility, those old rich families who now had no money. Gaius also gave to the equites eligibility to certain jury duties, a powerful function that had before been the exclusive right of the nobility.

Only the old landed aristocracy was against Gaius. The nouveaux riches and the people were for him. He had worked up all the elements of a popular tyrannical monarchy; the only thing he lacked was some way to secure his retention of office. Nonetheless, it was quite a start to have both of those classes on one's side.

Gaius also proposed sending people out to other areas to Romanize and build up markets and colonies in Africa.

What recourse was left to the nobility against this man? They could not get the approval of the people, but they could outbid him. Gaius protested that they were being unjust, that they were making too many concessions to the masses. The nobility asked the masses whether they preferred justice or more concessions. Gaius was abandoned by the Roman people; he was outbid by the nobles, and he died cursing the people that he had tried to help. The Greeks had warned him about the rabble, but they never told him how low it was.

The Gracchi had made a tremendous effort to correct civil law through natural law. But as Rostovtzeff observes:

> . . . they did not realize the difficulty and complexity of the situation; and it is unlikely that they foresaw the ultimate result of their revolutionary policy. Even if the

programme of the brothers had been completely carried out, it could hardly have sufficed to make a radical change in position. To set up at Rome a democracy of the Greek type was a dream or a farce, and to allot land even to every member of the proletariat could never bring back the time when the state rested securely upon a strong peasant population. (*Rome*, 104)

The application of the Greek criterion of justice to the civil area of Rome produced internal reforms that appeared handsome. But what criterion was to be applied to other nations in the provinces? Was the same criterion to be pronounced as absolute for other people as well? At first the Gracchi were just thinking about the Romans. They did not want to involve other people. But very gradually they were led to deal with other nations as well. For a time the negative attitude, that anything bad for the Senate was good for everyone, prevailed.

When Gaius auctioned taxation to the capitalists, what did it mean to the provinces? It meant the introduction of the worst kind of abuse of taxation. And if the local government rebelled, they would be put down by a Roman jury of capitalists, for the right to sit on the jury was also granted them. The few solitary Romans who stood up against this kind of abuse were welcomed as exiles in the provinces.

Rostovtzeff condemns the Gracchi approach as unrealistic. He says:

> They should have taken into account the power and influence of the highest classes, and recognized the fact that Rome was a world-wide power. The right course was to soften, not to exasperate, the feelings of classes, to devise new forms of government for the Roman empire, and not to galvanize into life the ancient democratic institutions of Greece. But this the Gracchi neither did nor even tried to do, and therefore action led to nothing but a prolonged and bloody conflict. (*Rome*, 104)

When Gaius Gracchus went down, the laws which

he had passed and the social consequences of these laws
did not go down. This was due to the Roman respect for
law. The aristocracy in crushing Gaius acted as did
Alexander when his army made demands upon him of
which he disapproved. He acquiesced to the army's demands, since to have not done so would have cost him the
good will of the army. But he singled out the leaders who
were responsible for those demands and had them executed. He made it plain thereby that he would be willing
to consider any future demands his army might have as
long as it sent to him, along with the demands, the men who
had conceived them.

The Roman aristocrats punished the leaders who
had drawn concessions from them, but they left the concessions untouched.

The division of classes that had emerged within
Rome with the Gracchi was permanent. It was an alignment
of classes in which the lower aristocrat was to associate
himself with the higher capitalist, while the highest noble
sought for support in the lowest classes.

The big task of the Roman land-owning aristocracy
was to try to separate the capitalists from the people. This
has been the problem of aristocracy throughout history. In
this contest for power it was to be the highest noble aligned
with the lowest classes who would finally prove victorious.

Rostovtzeff dwells on the reasons for the Roman
wars which followed the death of Gaius; he writes:

> Hoping, probably, to divert popular attention from the
> critical issues raised by the Gracchi, the Senate, immedi-
> ately after their victory at home, began a succession of
> foreign wars. These wars resembled the final campaign
> against Carthage. Their object was to promote the finan-
> cial interests of the large landowners who formed the
> ruling class, and to increase the territory of the Roman
> state in Gaul and Africa, as well as to draw away the
> attention of the people from domestic affairs. (*Rome*,
> 105)

There are many ways of dealing with domestic problems, but it is a certainty that the plan which proposes to deal with them by concentrating attention on external aggression will solve domestic problems with much greater speed than one which proposes peaceful means. It has been repeatedly illustrated in history how a have-not nation such as Hitler's Germany or Mussolini's Italy solved its domestic problems through external belligerence.

If, hypothetically, everyone in New York City went on a picnic and while everyone was away the city were blown up, the resulting ruin would be a great source of national prosperity. Think of all the opportunities for employment and capital investment it would provide when the task of reconstruction was begun. Is this not exactly what happens with all the ruined cities that follow in the wake of war? A bombed-out city is a great source of prosperity, not only to the people who rebuild it, but to its inhabitants who share in the fruits of reconstruction. On the sites of former conflagrations, new gleaming buildings arise. Italy is filled with ruined cities that were rebuilt after the second world war. It was not surprising to hear an Italian, envious of the construction going on in adjacent, more fortunate towns, ruefully complain that his town had not been touched by war.

Does the modern urge for slum clearance stem just from the desire to clear slums? Is it not really a logical way with which to create work projects and prosperity? Instead of an enemy blowing up our old buildings, we do it ourselves.

When a nation sends out expeditionary forces, as did the Romans after the fall of the Gracchi, it is really aiming at heightened prosperity at home.

An expeditionary force is a consumer market, with no work market. It creates immense opportunity for domestic wealth. Without the Crusades, Christendom would have amounted to nothing. The Crusades made Europe economically solvent. A great mass of moving men creates problems which can only be solved through economic production. Quarters have to be constructed to house them; ships have to be built to transport them across the seas; and an enormous variety of industries have to emerge to provide for their material needs. All this because of an expeditionary force!

In North Africa Jugurtha perceived the weakness of Rome. He became a genuine nuisance to Rome because Rome was very much like the United States of today, where the upper class has little mind for united action. The senatorial party in Rome had become divided and the small powers around the Mediterranean took advantage of the situation, even though there was no one big enough to threaten Rome. Jugurtha was a nuisance to Rome in the same way that Castro is a nuisance to the United States, because of the divided mind of the people in power.

Sallust portrays this period well, even though he was a partisan of the popular party and Julius Caesar against the Senate. What he says is fully consistent with Polybius.

Behind this division in Rome was something comparable to what occurred in France with Robespierre; there was no genuine foreign enemy. On this subject, Hegel writes:

> The Roman State, drawing its resources from rapine, came to be rent asunder by quarrels about dividing the spoils. For the first occasion of the breaking out of contention within it, was the legacy of Attalus, King of Pergamus, who had bequeathed his treasures to the Roman State. (*Philosophy of History*, 309)

Tiberius Gracchus suggested the spoils be divided according to Greek justice. Since Rome had conquered the world, Gracchus proposed an equal distribution of conquered wealth. But the Senate protested. This had never been done before. And now that the Senate had a chance of taking the lion's share, Gracchus wanted to deprive it of its loot.

On all sides men were making proposals. Some wanted to keep the senate strong, some wanted to let the equites run things, and some suggested a rebellion of the proletariat. Every Roman had an idea of what to do, now that Rome was without an enemy.

It was easy enough to propose an idea, but how was one going to get other people, who also had ideas of their own, to listen to it? The whole problem of Rome became: How to get the people to submit? Tiberius Gracchus tried to be democratic. Hegel observes at this point: "Ruin now broke in unchecked, and as there existed no generally recognized and absolutely essential object to which the country's energy could be devoted, individualities and physical force were in the ascendant. The enormous corruption of Rome displays itself in the war with Jugurtha." (*Philosophy of History*, 309)

In order to have one's ideas heard, what price did one have to pay? The price of financing an army. A man could then say that he had not only an idea but also an army and his idea would be listened to. Many ideas are projected at the United Nations but until it has an army with which to make itself heard, few will listen.

Even Marius hesitated. He did not want an army; he would have rather persuaded the Romans. But Julius Caesar was to come and say that if you do not want to save Rome, put the army down.

The division between the Optimates and the Populares made possible the rise of Jugurtha and Mithradites, and the Cimbri and the Teutons. Marius rose to power because he proved his abilities in the Jugurtha campaign. He was the son of a farmer and began his career with a nobleman for his benefactor, and therefore leaned to the Optimates.

The nobility usually finds it safer to have men of superior talent from the lower classes on its side. The nobleman bears a title and the title represents a function. If a man from the lower classes can be trained to assist him in carrying out his function, the nobleman while being spared some of his arduous duties can more comfortably enjoy the prestige of his title.

When the nobility loses its function, it defensively closes ranks and excludes the people of talent whom it might have formerly employed. And it is this excluded talent which becomes its bitterest enemy.

At the beginning of his career, Marius championed the cause of the Optimates, but when the Optimates sneered at his plebeian ancestors, he gradually came to realize that his particular talents could be used to best advantage on behalf of the Populares. He began his career in the military service of his benefactor Metellus, and he was given a high rank in the campaign against Jugurtha in North Africa.

The attitude that prevailed in Rome and made the Jugurtha incident possible is best expressed by the phrase: "What's in it for me?" Elevated to the political plane, it becomes: "You have an excellent plan, but what's in it for my constituents?"

This disposition was not only profitable to the Romans, but to the foreigner who cared to exploit it.

Jugurtha, who was able to raise fabulous wealth from the pockets of his submissive subjects, could buy off large numbers of Roman senators. He made the boast that if he had enough wealth he could buy Rome itself.

Rome was filled with ambitious men. If a man is ambitious, he may come to feel that the scope given to his abilities in his own country is too narrow. Such a man would not hesitate to hire himself out to another country if by doing so his talents could find wider expression. The Athenians had done this.

When men of talent are reduced to writing letters to the editors of *The New York Times*, they had better be watched carefully. Jugurtha played on the ambitions of the talented Roman.

Marius, discontent in North Africa, returned to Rome to make a bid to launch his political career. Marius was an intelligent man, but he saw through the educated approach. He found that rough talk worked better when certain things had to be done. He disparaged his opponents for reading Greek books to find solutions to problems, which he boasted he could solve by drawing on his own experience. His bid succeeded and his old benefactor was relieved from his command in North Africa. Then Marius went to North Africa to get Jugurtha. Unfortunately, he had with him a young aide by the name of Sulla.

Sulla, who in being kind to some prisoners had made friends among the enemy, dared to go with a handful of men to the camp of the African king, Bocchus, who was sheltering Jugurtha. Jugurtha had become quite desperate by then and had been reduced to commando warfare against the Romans. Sulla walked into the camp surrounded by Jugurtha's forces and had Jugurtha surrendered to him. Marius got the credit for Jugurtha's capture. Sulla had a medallion engraved, which was circulated widely in Rome, showing Jugurtha being led into slavery by Sulla.

When Marius returned to Rome, he had an army.

Mommsen reminds us that Marius built an interesting army. The old Roman method for staffing an army was unsatisfactory because it was hard to persuade the Romans to leave their farms to join the army.

What kind of an army arose during the time of Marius and Sulla? It was a new army made up of people who could not afford to supply their own arms, as the soldiers of the old army did. The arms were given to them instead. The difference between an army that is comprised of men who supply their own equipment and one that is made up of men who do not supply their own equipment, is that the former are anxious to return to civilian life, whereas the latter are men who never would amount to anything in civilian life and are anxious to stay in the army where they can enjoy an otherwise unattainable prestige.

This new kind of army could have never beaten Hannibal, but it was adequate for keeping the Romans from tearing themselves apart.

When peace returned, Marius had a choice of saying that he had a plan as well as an army to back it, or of following the methods of the Gracchi. He chose the latter.

To achieve political power, he had to associate himself with two types of popular leaders, the popular leader from the aristocracy and the popular leader from the lower classes.

The popular leader from the aristocracy was the young aristocrat who had inherited his wealth and was anxious to make a final gesture on behalf of the people before he was reduced to oblivion.

The popular leader from the lower classes was the Senator McCarthy type who could never have gotten the support of the upper classes and who derived his power from constant agitation. These popular leaders from the lower classes succeeded in having many laws passed dividing the Cimbri lands. But their power still rested on agitation. They were sharks in a goldfish bowl, and finally Marius turned against them. He slaughtered his own supporters and along with them, his domestic program. The popular leaders, the rabble-rousers, succeeded in doing what the Senate could never do: they separated the people from the capitalists.

In the east, Mithradates, king of Pontus, who would have never dared to face an earlier Rome on the march, called for a war.

Sulla had an army similar to that of Marius, and he was given the job of meeting this new threat. Sulla's army was not a mercenary army, but an army of people who were promised a share in the commonwealth which they had not earned.

While Sulla was in southern Italy, Cinna, a new popular leader, arose in Rome. Cinna then brought Marius back to Rome and gave him the command for the eastern expedition, sending a message to Sulla advising him to come back home. Truman sent a similar message to MacArthur but when MacArthur came home, he left his army behind.

Sulla pondered Cinna's message and submitted it to his army. His men agreed that he should obey and go back home, only they would go along with him.

The result of the peace that came from the destruction of Carthage was a Roman army made up of Roman soldiers marching on Rome. Marius fled Rome to have some colorful adventures in exile, as described by Plutarch. Sulla returned to Rome where he straightened matters out. But he did not stay long because he knew that if he did, his army, impatient for the expedition in the east, would have probably withdrawn its support for him. Sulla left with his army for the east; Rome had its first bloodbath. Sulla's supporters were exterminated by the supporters of Marius.

Sulla has been treated badly by historians. He never made nice speeches that might have endeared him to historians, as did Henry V before he became a good king. Mommsen observes:

> he also called things by their right name with brutal frankness. Thus he has irreparably offended the great mass of the weak-hearted who are more revolted at the name than at the thing. (*History of Rome*, 198)

His technique of proscription offends more than Marxian class war. His approach has nowhere in history proven successful in settling class wars. The idea that by completely liquidating the dissenting class one will get rid of dissension is impracticable. Even Sulla did not go far enough to accomplish this end. He was finally prevailed upon to relax his liquidations.

Sulla never tried to cloak his conduct under the word justice. He simply said that what he did was for the welfare of the state.

One is reminded of Sulla by a statement attributed to Thomas Cromwell who directed that a political prisoner be taken out for trial and execution. Cromwell was minister of Henry VIII and the founder of a strong English state. His technique, like Sulla's, was to clean up all the opposition very quickly. Since the opposition happened to be Catholic and an endless argument between Protestants and Catholics was inevitable, he arranged to kill all the good Catholics and leave only the inferior ones to protest. It was unlikely that their protest would be too effective.

Cromwell acted like a surgeon who, realizing that a diseased organ must be removed, proceeded to cut it out, over the objections of his patient, who might have had a fond attachment to that organ. The king would turn to Cromwell to ask who it was that should be removed. Among Cromwell's victims was Thomas More, a man who would have been a good citizen, but who merely objected to the religious maneuvering that was going on. Cromwell has been conveniently forgotten.

Sulla's disposition is similar to the one which accompanied the French Revolution. His attitude might be compared to Thomas Paine's rebuttal of Burke, when he accused Burke, who was horrified at what happened to the royalty of France, of fussing about the plumes when the bird was dead.

The leaders of the French Revolution assembled, pondered what had to be done, and decided it was necessary to slaughter the opposition, and even the slayer himself, should he be reluctant. But their solution, under the banner of liberty, equality, and fraternity, was, after all, idealistic. Mommsen says of Sulla that there was a certain cynical frankness about him.

Rostovtzeff, in commenting on Sulla, says:

> Sulla's motives . . . were not merely cruelty and the desire to consolidate his personal authority. In exterminating the Samnites his intention was to put an end to the Italian war, and he believed that the reign of terror was inevitable, if Italy was to be thoroughly unified and Latinized. His measures were effective: there is no doubt that the almost complete extermination of the Samnites

hastened the process of Latinization in south Italy. But was there no other possible method? To Latinize the desert into which a large part of the Samnites country had been converted was no difficult task. (*Rome*, 113)

A comparable example is Israel. Let us see if she can find some other way to Israelize the Arabs. The Arabs are a desperate people. Their religion, Mohammedanism, is a desperate religion. The Arab when cornered will never give up his faith.

What Sulla did was necessary. It is difficult to assess a man unless the motives for his actions are fully understood. With most historical figures, the motives for their actions cannot be too clearly understood since they are rarely realized. Most men die dissatisfied. Marius died dissatisfied. Tiberius and Gaius Gracchus died dissatisfied. There are not too many people in history who did what they wanted to do before they died. But Sulla, at the height of his powers, content in what he had achieved, retired from the political scene to die satisfied.

The absoluteness of his power is illustrated by Plutarch:

There was nothing lacking in the tremendous power Sulla gathered together in the circus . . . [prisoners] to the number of six thousand, and just as he commenced speaking to the senate, in the temple of Bellona, proceeded to cut them down, by men appointed for that service. The cry of so vast a multitude put to the sword, in so narrow a space, was naturally heard some distance, and startled the senators. He, however, continuing his speech with a calm and unconcerned countenance, bade them listen to what he had to say, and not busy themselves with what was doing out of doors; he had given directions for the chastisement of some offenders.

Sulla wielded at the end of his career a power which he willingly put aside when he was content with his achievement.

What had he achieved?

He had restored the Senate and attempted to cripple democracy forever. His revision of the constitution included the necessity of clearing any proposal that the lower assembly might consider through the Senate. This in effect annulled the Hortensian law of 287 B.C. which had given Rome a double legislature. Rome had had two houses, both of which could legislate. This arrangement had been the result of tremendous social pressures. There had been two main assemblies, the general assembly (Centuriate Assembly) which included the plebeians but was deliberately weighted in favor of the aristocracy, and the assembly of the plebeians themselves. It was the powers of the lower assembly that were annulled by Sulla.

Further, no magistrate could now be re-elected to the same post for a period of 10 years. This measure made it impossible for any man to rise continuously to power, as Marius and Gaius Gracchus had done. Sulla intended to safeguard liberty by restraining the higher offices, and putting an age limit on them.

Any man who held the office of tribune could not be elected to a higher office in the state. This would be as if Congress passed a law stating that anyone who had held the office of Governor of New York or California was not eligible for the presidency. The effect this would have on the quality of future holders of those offices would be comparable to the effect Sulla intended his measure to have on the quality of the tribunes. They would become mediocre men who entertained no high personal ambitions.

These were big reforms. Sulla was trying to restore the hegemony of the Centuriate Assembly, which meant the restoration to power of the aristocracy. But not many of the old aristocrats were left. He had to create, therefore, new ranks among the aristocracy. Sulla was not favoring any particular class. What he was trying to preserve was the old system of checks and balances, which Polybius and Panaetius had taught Scipio was necessary to save the state.

In order to reconstitute the Senate he reached into the equestrian class, taking equites and making senators out of them. Sulla's revision of the constitution was an evidence of the application of the reason of the *ius naturale* to Roman law. It was an effort to create a governmental structure that could survive the individuals who held power in it.

Sulla forced into law the Roman tradition which prescribed the duration and sequence of offices a man might hold in his political career. He forced the magistrate to move from one office to another prescribed office, taking all the necessary steps instead of side-stepping certain offices in a short cut to power. He tried to set up a system of government which no rational Roman would criticize. Sulla was not the champion of the Senate. He had made it plain that the Senate could be crushed just as the people could be. The instant he released the pressure on the state, his enemies rebelled against him. He would have defeated his own end had he retained his absolute power. But he did not retain it.

Appian did not sympathize with this brutal man but marveled that Sulla had laid down his power. He pointed out that Sulla was the first and only man to abdicate his power without compulsion. He did not even arrange to make his power hereditary to his sons. After Sulla, there was a scramble for his power which Pompey ultimately won only by repudiating Sulla's constitution.

Appian observed that Sulla had killed many people, and that there were not many people alive in Rome who did not have some relative whose death they could blame on him. Yet Sulla proclaimed himself a private citizen and retired contentedly to his farm at Cunnae. It is true that Sulla had a vast army of faithful friends. He had been generous. He had freed many men from slavery, he had adopted as members of his family 30,000 ex-slaves, who bore his name, the Cornelii. When a society is reorganized, it is nice to have friends. But by laying down his power he exposed himself to retribution. Political assassinations are usually the result not of calculating noblemen, who have to be assured of their personal safety before they will strike, but of the little man who is perfectly willing to die for his act.

Sulla knew he was accostable. In fact, he said that if at any time anyone wanted to discuss his past actions with him, he would be perfectly willing to discuss them. He believed that what he had done was rational. Of his opponents he would ask, what would they have done for the welfare of the state if they had been confronted with the results of the actions of Gaius and Tiberius?

But in our discussion, he would say, let us be rational and talk not of personalities but of the rational needs of the state.

Sulla could ask: why did Mithradates, who had tried to revive the ancient Persian wars between east and west, arise to challenge Rome? Had not Mithradates, with the help of the rabble of underprivileged Greeks in the east, wiped out tremendous numbers of Romans? Had not this disaster shaken Rome with an economic crisis that was reported by Cicero in a speech to the Senate? Why was it possible for the Greeks to slaughter all the Romans in the east? The reason for this disaster was at home. It was the civil war that raged in Italy, which like a cancer had to be cut out. Why had the gladiators rebelled? Why had Sertorius risen to power in Spain? Why was there piracy everywhere? The crucial problem was to make Rome strong.

Those who think Caesar was a monster, what do they imagine Brutus, his assassin, would have done had he been given Caesar's power? He would have done the same thing Sulla did.

After his retirement Sulla, according to Appian, was accosted only once, and this by a little boy. Sulla, who had opposed the greatest men of his time with towering rage was followed home one night, through the streets of Rome, by a little boy who reviled him for what he had done.

Sulla calmly ignored the angry youth till he reached his home and then, turning to a friend, he pointed to the boy and remarked that it is because of this young man that no one will ever again lay down his power as he had done. Appian said that Sulla retired from the scene to his own estate because he was weary of war, weary of power, weary of Rome.

He had attempted to freeze the constitution. The Romans were indeed going to freeze the constitution, so well that a time would come when the structure of the government would survive the Romans and the offices of state would pass out of Roman to German hands.

Sulla had tried it with the republican constitution. He had striven to create offices that would survive their personnel. His work lasted for the short time of ten years, and it was destroyed by the very man whom he had prepared to perpetuate it.

Hegel describes the period which had created a Sulla in these words:

> We thus see the most terrible and dangerous powers arising against Rome; yet the military force of this state is victorious over all. Great individuals now appear on the stage as during the times of the fall of Greece. The biographies of Plutarch are here also of the deepest interest. It was from the disruption of the state, which had no longer any consistency or firmness in itself, that these colossal individualities arose, instinctively impelled to restore that political unity which was no longer to be found in men's dispositions. It is their misfortune that they cannot maintain a pure morality, for their course of action contravenes things as they are, and is a series of transgressions. Even the noblest, the Gracchi, were not merely the victims of injustice and violence from without, but were themselves involved in corruption and wrong that universally prevailed. But that which these individuals propose and accomplish, has on its side the higher sanction of the World-Spirit, and must eventually triumph. The idea of an organization for the vast empire

being altogether absent, the Senate could not assert the authority of government. The sovereignty was made dependent on the people — that people which was now a mere mob, and was obliged to be supported by corn from the Roman provinces. We should refer to Cicero to see how all affairs of state were decided in riotous fashion, and with arms in hand, by the wealth and power of the grandees on the one side, and by the troops of rabble on the other. (*Philosophy of History*, 310-311)

The Romans were, during this period, becoming a class of men who wanted peace and order, but they were harassed on all sides by enemies aware of their weakness. Pirates dominated their seas flamboyantly in their golden ships, with purple sails and silver oars, jeering at Roman power.

Rome was divided, and it lacked a formidable external enemy. What would have happened if a Ghenghis Kahn had suddenly appeared at the head of a vast horde? Rome would have probably risen to meet him in the competitive cooperative way it had met Hannibal. The only thing that could have united Rome would have been such an enemy.

But Carthage, like a dead horse, was no more, and the maggots that thrived on the carcass were not badly off. They might even have rebelled against resistance to a formidable enemy if it involved weapons that might sear them, like our atomic bombs. So men arose who tried to change things; but a man who tries to change things is always considered immoral.

They tried to make the people cooperate. But why should the people cooperate in competition? Had not the whole world been conquered? How paralyzing would our strikes be, what crowds would one see in Times Square, if we were ever to lose our enemy!

In Rome there had been two groups, the Populares, who having achieved all for which it had been striking and cooperating, now wanted to rule, and the senatorial Optimates, who kept shouting to the mob that it was not fit to rule. Sulla had abolished the functions of the censor, since he did not want his newly appointed senators removed before they had had time to get the necessary training in affairs of state.

The people of Rome were fit to rule only in will, not knowledge. The Senate itself was not fit to rule either; it had been good in times of wars against enemies, but now it had no enemy.

A politician today in his climb to power must utilize the two chief forces in our society: money and heads. Politics, as someone has said, is the art of getting votes from the poor and money from the rich to protect each from the other.

During this period this was exactly what happened. People were coming forward to protect the rich from the poor and the poor from the rich, but mostly in search of personal advantage. Sallust refers to them as demagogues, men ostensibly upholding the senate or the commons, but actually assailing the government, showing neither self-restraint nor moderation.

Sulla knew this aspect of Roman politics had to be overcome. His constitution required an additional quality, which he hoped to give it by laying aside his power and letting his people see that it was necessary to accept the constitution on its own terms. He hoped, by this act, to give the constitution authority. He wanted to show the people what it meant not to be ambitious. For this reason he also treated someone else with respect; for no apparent reason his favorite was Pompey.

Plutarch writes:

> For as soon as Sulla saw him [Pompey] advancing, his army so well appointed . . . he alighted from his horse and being first, as was his due, saluted by them with the title of Imperator, he returned the salutation upon Pompey . . . which might well cause surprise, as none could have anticipated that he could have imparted, to one so young in years and not yet a senator, a title which

was the object of contention between him and the Scipios and Marii . . . which he was rarely seen to do with anyone else, notwithstanding that there were many about him of great rank and honor.

Sulla's treatment of Pompey gave to Pompey an importance and a dignity that survived Sulla's death. Sulla never made him appear as a lackey, which he could have easily done.

To oblige Sulla, Pompey had gotten rid of his own wife and married a woman of Sulla's choice. Sulla offered this same test to Julius Caesar, but Caesar refused to comply.

Plutarch says:

After Sulla became master of Rome, he wished to make Caesar put away his wife Cornelia, daughter of Cinna, the late sole ruler of the commonwealth, but was unable to effect it either by promises or intimidation . . . and in consultation whether he should be put to death, when it was urged by some that it was not worth his while to contrive the death of a boy, he answered, that they knew little who did not see more than one Marius in that boy.

His prediction was not verified, for although Caesar began as an Adlai Stevenson of the progressive movement, he finally did what Sulla had wanted to do. He, Caesar, did it so well that freedom was lost.

Pompey was groomed by Sulla to be the object of authority. If he would restore in the Romans the disposition to obey, Sulla felt that he had given them a workable constitution with which they would survive. The truth is that his system would not have worked; it was a republican system based on freedom.

Had the opponents of Caesar been able to save it, then it would have been another historical instance of the famous "twice" of Hegel. It would have proved that at their first opportunity the people lacked insight into what was necessary, but given a second chance, they supported it.

Sulla gave them their first opportunity, and it was

undone by Pompey. It was impossible to maintain Sulla's
constitution. It would have been preserved only had he not
laid down his power. But it would have lost the quality of
freedom he was trying to restore. Sulla would have been
another Augustus.

Augustus, who disguised his absolute rule behind
proper constitutional forms, has been accused of draining
the constitution of all power. But what alternative did he
have? The only other thing he could have done would have
been to lay down his power, as Sulla had, and the results of
his abdication would have been the same as with Sulla.
Sulla's intention was to give freedom one more try. He
would lay down his power and see if this wonderful republican heritage the Romans had enjoyed for so many centuries could survive. Sulla must have made this gesture to
please a woman. Only a sweet moment could have exacted
a concession like this from so tough a man.

After Sulla died, the whole thing started again.

Pompey could not simply step into Sulla's place.
Sulla had outlawed that. He had merely groomed Pompey
as a personality. The only avenue for Pompey to travel was
through the cycle of public offices, which Sulla had made
mandatory for the statesman. Pompey went through this
cycle. It was a period of humility; everyone trusted him.

Pompey may be accused of being too slow in grasp-
ing at the opportunity of upsetting Sulla's constitution
sooner than he did. But this does not mean he was not
ambitious. He was a very ambitious man. A very ambitious
man is usually very cautious. If he really has his heart set on
something, it is very hard to take chances with it.

If a man wants to be a great general, he has to
expose himself to risks as a lieutenant. There is only one
god that governs greatness in this world, luck. But the
lieutenant might protest. Why should he risk his life as a
lieutenant when he wants to risk it as a general?

The man who wants to keep his light under a bushel

till the right moment, will keep his light under a bushel forever, and devote his declining years to counseling the youth to keep their light under a bushel until the right moment.

Sulla's reformed constitution really put the Senate in charge of the government. And it was in charge because it included everyone who had governmental experience. But the people wanted to be in charge, too. Because of the Gracchian reforms, the people wanted to have a say in policy.

The Senate of Rome wanted as its instrument a military leader who would not lead an army back to Rome. Pompey ingratiated himself to the people as well as to the Senate. At first, his task was to get the approval of the Senate; the people's approval was a simple matter.

The difference between Caesar's command and Pompey's command was that Pompey could not make a decision without lengthy senatorial discussion interfering with it, whereas the instant Caesar made a decision his troops marched. While Pompey was helplessly listening to committee reports, Caesar moved. The Senate was filled with men who had ideas on how things should be done, and these men were looking around for a man to help with their talents. The man who would eventually succeed in Rome would be the one who would disregard all this advice. But Sulla said a good man must listen to the Senate, and poor Pompey kept listening. Sulla after all had intended the state to operate on a basis of civil freedom.

Lepidus and the elder Brutus attempted to undo Sulla's reform. Pompey was sent out as an aide to Catullus to defeat Lepidus.

Catullus was the actual commander in the fight against Lepidus. After the defeat of Lepidus near Rome, the hope of the anti-Sullans was transferred to Sertorius in Spain. Luck really reached out for Pompey, and it seemed to be the luck of Sulla, reaching from beyond the grave. It was as if Sulla had had so much luck that he could lavish it on his favorite, like a Christian saint, even after death.

Lepidus joined Sertorius, but died shortly after.

Sertorius was a truly fascinating figure. A member of the Marian party, he withdrew to Spain where he started to do what Hannibal had done. He also set up a counter Roman state, having the formal structure of Rome itself.

Pompey was sent to assist Mettelus against Sertorius. Sertorius was unbeatable. He could raise armies from people with whom he had nothing in common. Sertorius was betrayed and assassinated, and the glory of a victory he had not won went to Pompey. While the campaign in Spain was drawing to a close and Rome was engaged in the second Mithradatic war, Spartacus rose in Italy, illustrating the unfailing Roman luck for synchronizing wars.

Spartacus was a Thracian commander of general status who led the revolt of the slaves. What was the reason for his rise to power? He rose in Italy because of the unwillingness of the Italians (the lack of will that General Walker keeps talking about). When there is a lack of will, any band of riffraff can rise up. Spartacus attracted all kinds of allies. He had quite a following. (He had the attraction of a Jack Dempsey or a Joe Louis.) He would have been able to lead his forces back to Thrace, but his followers preferred to stay in Italy. They kept wondering why the cowardly Romans should be living in luxury.

Roman armies had to be sent after them, but they were defeated. Spartacus had been a nuisance to a very prosperous society. The battles that were fought were over luxury, not poverty.

Crassus, one of Sulla's officers, was chosen as commander of a new army and actually won the campaigns. He broke the back of the army of Spartacus. But Pompey, who had joined him very late in the campaign, again got the glory for rooting out the enemy. Pompey's luck was still following him.

Pompey camped outside of Rome and refused to disband his army until the Senate approved his request to run for consul. He was making use of what Sulla did not want him to make use of, approval. For all this, he used his power modestly. He might have retained his army. He was allowed to run for consul. He was after all the savior of Italy.

Crassus was a very rich man. He had made a tremendous fortune during Sulla's proscriptions. Poor Sulla! He wanted to kill only the people who deserved to die. But a man's property could get him on Sulla's proscription lists. The story is told of the old farmer who, examining the latest list and finding his name on it, said, "my farm has destroyed me." It became dangerous to have property. The people who owned property started to unload it.

Crassus was at hand to buy out all these unwanted estates. He hurried the process by setting fire to buildings in Rome and then dispatching his private fire brigades to put out the fire, giving him an occasion to buy out the burned-out owner. He even held his brigades off if the owner did not want to sell, pointing out as the property burned that he was perfectly willing to purchase it while it still had value, but that its value was diminishing as they talked. It must be said of Crassus that in a society whose laws were not functioning too well, he did provide the nucleus of an efficient fire department.

Crassus came back to Rome with Pompey and his army[24].

The Senate did not think too much of Crassus. This was a mistake. He would have been a good tool, anxious as he was to court the aristocracy. But the Senate insisted on having the best. Pompey was elected as consul and Crassus was elected also, a kind of vice-president who rode to office on Pompey's coat tails. But Pompey failed to get the cooperation of the Senate. They denied his veterans the pensions that Pompey had promised them. The popular party took advantage of this rift, offering to back Pompey's demands if he would restore the power of the plebiscite. This meant restoring the full power of the tribune.

In 70 B.C. Pompey did just this, and the Sullan constitution was abolished, ten years after it was instituted. It was easier to get popular support for his policies than senatorial support. He also acceded to other demands by restoring the equestrians to jury courts.

Cicero now became involved in politics, as a state prosecutor. He appeared as a popular-type conservative leader who was for the people. He was an eloquent man who needed large audiences. Whereas the intelligentsia often failed to perceive who had won a discussion, the listening populace always recognized the winner.

Cicero had not made up his mind which side he was really on. But he began his career by supporting the transfer of knights to the courts and colonies.

Cicero was the first and last real Roman philosopher. He translated Plato's *Republic* and six of Plato's dialogues into Latin. He invented the Roman vocabulary. But even he apologizes for this work, saying that it was not really important, being valuable rather for talkers than for doers.

In Rome, Pompey wondered how he was going to retain his power if the constitution continued to work and he was deprived of his army.

The armies of Pompey and Crassus were stationed outside of Rome. In order to maintain the spirit of armies, it is necessary to give them something to do. Pompey had a few of his political colleagues introduce legislation. The first law passed authorized the wiping out of piracy in the Mediterranean.

Piracy had become a great money-making operation. It was an "over the counter" market. A wealthy man could invest in a pirate ship or two. The pirates were being financed by wealthy people. This is not so strange. All great enterprises begin mistily. Had not the Elizabethan English found great glory in capturing gold mines disguised as Spanish galleons? Had not Thucydides pointed out that every state in the beginning starts with piracy and that the leading pirate must go straight and become a pirate police-man?

Had not St. Augustine said that the leading pirates are going straight whether they know it or not? Pompey got the command to cope with the pirate menace and in an incredibly short time swept the pirates from the seas. The pirates were never pirates afterwards. Pompey hired them and put them to work; and to discourage their maritime activities, he had their leading centers moved safely inland.

Every time there was a lull, the east rose in an effort to realize its lingering dream of rebuilding the Persian Empire. Lucullus had been stationed there since 74. But he had become unpopular in Rome because his stoical sense of justice made it hard for the Romans to move into the east and do what they wanted. Lucullus restrained the Romans too much. So the popular assembly in Rome had him removed from his command, and he returned to lead his life of Lucullan luxury.

Lucullus was a great epicurean stoic. He lived in an eclectic age. After he was removed from command, he gave Lucullan dinners, a term one never uses unless one is prepared to spend a lot of money.

Lucullus was a kind of Rockefeller Foundation. One could hardly object to him. He gave people libraries to read in and had the best Greeks in his house.

The second law that Pompey's colleagues passed assigned to him Lucullus' command, not of the army alone, but also the command at sea.

Mithradates was living too long and his son became impatient. It is not always good for a ruler to last too long. Louis XIV lasted too long and his reign caused great trouble for France. So the son of Mithradates rose up against his father, and his despondent father committed suicide.

Pompey went to the east, crushed the resistance and marched to Syria and as far as Palestine, making the entire area subject to Rome in 63 B.C. He took time in returning to Rome, not coming back until 61 B.C.

In Pompey's absence, Caesar, Cicero, Cataline, and the younger Cato had risen, all personalities that appear in the lives of Plutarch. The most interesting figure was Caesar. Six years younger than Pompey, born in 100 B.C. and related to Marius, who had been his uncle, Caesar had been making speeches extolling his poor aunt and outlining her suffering. He was also related to Cinna, through marriage with Cinna's daughter. He began his career as an eloquent orator. He attacked Dollabella, whose great crime was that he was rich. Caesar's skillful prosecution marked him as a man who was going to go places. He won what might be called a Rhodes scholarship. He went to Rhodes and was captured by a band of pirates, who found him to be an amusing hostage, always kidding with them and good-naturedly telling them he would send them to the gallows. Caesar later kept his word.

Caesar returned to Rome and was elected as a quaestor and continued to make speeches about his Aunt Julia. He also raised monuments to Marius, which was quite a thing to do, living under Sulla's constitution.

Julius Caesar was a demagogue, a popular leader of the rabble, until he finally realized when he was about 40 years old that his methods would not work. He had the same objects in view as Gaius Gracchus, and used the same methods. He tried them all. He is referred to as the greatest genius of antiquity because when he realized that he had to become a general, he learned how to be a general.

It is because of Caesar's work as a general that Europe has the form it has today. This was his most important contribution. A testimony to his genius is the protective wall he built in ten years around the Roman empire, which enabled Roman pacifism to survive 500 years.

The arrangements he made with brutality and magnanimity created a situation where Germanic tribes were always at odds with each other, taking turns at proudly defending Roman frontiers against one another, while the Romans lost the will to defend themselves. It was to take 500 years for the Germanic tribes to get fed up with themselves fighting on both sides, and to realize that by merely uniting together they could take Rome. But the Roman system, instituted by Caesar, functioned all this time without even trying.

Caesar was a great spender, working on the premise that a man who is afraid of debt will never make friends. The populace liked to watch him in action. They liked to see his innocent victims squirm. He knew that his approach to matters of state would involve him in trouble, so he tried to get elected to the priestly order, which would have conferred on him inviolability. But the Senate blocked his election. He was never tempted to try to win the Senate's favor. He came from the highest family but always pleaded the cause of the populace. He was a popular radical leader, uncompromising against the Senate. At one point the Senate tried to implicate him in the Cataline conspiracy.

The Cataline conspiracy was a sign of discontent on all sides comparable to the message of our avant-garde, which keeps proclaiming that the whole country is rotten from top to bottom. Cataline represents an extraordinary moment when people from all sides flocked to join him, and his propaganda would shift, day after day, accommodating all class interests. It illuminated the peril of the state. Rostovteff reminds us that

> the years of Pompey's absence were years of feverish attempt on the part of the democrats to make themselves, by hook or by crook, masters of the situation at Rome. They had once before made use of an aristocrat to gain their ends, and they were prepared to repeat the same trick. They found a suitable tool in L. Sergius Catalina, a ruined aristocrat, a man of great ambition, who possessed no small influence among the impoverished young nobles and also among the dregs of society at Rome. He had quarreled with the Senate and was

ready to serve Caesar and his party, if they would smooth his way to the consulship. (*Rome*, 122-123)

The most dangerous members of the lower class are the men from the ruined upper class. Cataline was such a man. He was a capable man but an evil man. He attempted to vie with Cicero for the consulship. Rostovteff continues:

> The mediator between the Senate and the knights was M. Tullius Cicero . . . who had just started his political career on the democratic side by attacking the senatorial juries and the senatorial misgovernment of the provinces . . . Cicero was ambitious . . . he wished to reach the highest position in that state . . . he dreamed of a reconciliation between the two highest classes of Roman society. Thus he was ready for a compact with the Senate; and against Cataline, a deserter from the aristocrats, the Senate put forward Cicero, a deserter from the democrats. (*Rome*, 123)

There was here a reversal of sides: a fallen aristocrat joined the populares, and a popular leader shifted to the senatorial side. The aristocratic type is a dangerous man. He thinks he is unequal but when he is forced to be equal, he dreams of revolution. He is dangerous because he is willing to stand his ground and die.

The source of political rule is that those who are not ready to die will submit to those who are ready to die. Cataline had a real willingness to die, whereas Cicero had not. Cataline vied with Cicero but Cicero won.

The only genuine popular leader of this time was Caesar. He had been committed to the popular cause from the very beginning, with never a temptation to shift sides. Lenin made the observation that the way to make big moves is to take up one cause and stick with it, never wavering. This was the procedure of Julius Caesar. Almost everyone at this time was wavering. Cataline seized upon the opportunity of this wavering. Caesar, who had backed Cataline initially, withdrew his support. Cataline, after he had been beaten, decided not to accept defeat. All about him he saw weakness. But he underestimated the orations of Cicero. The speeches of Cicero against Cataline are monuments of oratory. Cicero, confronted with a man who clearly intends to overthrow the government, asks:

> How much further, Cataline, will you abuse our forbearance? How much longer will your recklessness baffle our restraint? Will your unbridled audacity stop at nothing? Do the night watches on the Palatine, the sentinels posted in the city leave you indifferent? Are you not moved by the alarm of the people, the rallying of all good men, the precautions of this meeting, the look and expressions of all assembled here? Can't you see your plot is exposed, don't you realize that all of us here assembled know the details of your conspiracy?[25]

The conspiracy of Cataline was revealed imprudently by one of Cataline's henchmen to his woman whose affections he was trying to win. He promised her that soon he would be able to give her that house upon the sea. Appian relates the incident thus:

> These facts were still secret when they were communicated to Cicero by Fulvia, a woman of position. Her lover, Quintus Curtius, had been expelled from the Senate for scandalous behavior, and merited inclusion in Cataline's party. With lighthearted braggadocio, he intimated to his mistress that he would soon be in a position of' power.

Sallust, who had insight into the times, records some of the speeches of Cataline to his men. Cataline played on their emotions. He pointed out that there were men with wealth in Rome; what were they doing? Were they beautifying the city? No. They were building villas on the sea and leveling mountains for villas in the mountains. The Roman rich had their Atlantic cities and their Adirondacks. Cataline's main point was that fortune offers all things and that splendid are the spoils of war. He asked his men to use him either as a leader or a soldier in the ranks. This is the line of thought of all leaders who have what they consider to be a good cause. Their followers are slaves of the good cause, and they the leaders are slaves of the slaves of the good cause. This was the position of a later Roman pontiff who called himself a slave of the slaves of God. Sallust goes on to say that Cataline's words fell on the ears of men who had no prospects for the future. Cataline promised them cancellation of debts, proscriptions, and all the other spoils of war. Personal interests were absolute. There was a confounding of right and left. His followers were rabble as well as former aristocrats. This illustrates how confounded class issues had become at this time. His plan was to utilize whatever hostility could be found in Rome. He had two camps. One was in the city and one was outside with the main army. The internal group in Rome was captured and put on trial.

During the trial it was proposed to execute these people. But protests were raised that this was not constitutional. It was not what could be legally done. It was argued that a man should not be declared a public enemy because he merely intended to dominate Rome through competition.

Caesar was at this trial, and he spoke against capital punishment for the conspirators. He addressed the fathers of the Senate and cautioned them not to let their feelings stand in the way. When the intellect is applied, he said, one prevails, but passions make one impotent. Napoleon read Caesar's speech carefully.[26]

Caesar reminded the senators that throughout the Punic Wars the Romans had never blindly retaliated but had asked what conduct would conform to dignity. He asked them to consider whether all men were really allowed the same freedom in their actions. That which the humble do is known only to a few, but that which those with great power do is known to all the world. In the highest station there is least freedom of action. What in lesser men is wrath, in a ruler is insolence and ruthlessness. These thoughts of Caesar were so nicely stated that it is easy to overlook how Machiavellian they were. Machiavelli usually gives the impression of speaking with a cynical sneer. Caesar reminds us, however, that when a man is in a lofty station, he must be restrained.

He advised that there were other laws with which to punish the conspirators. They could be permitted to go into exile. If one insisted on making the punishment rigorous to match the infamy of the intended deed, why not skin them alive? The big question a state must answer when it has an Eichmann in its power is, what policy should be followed to the greatest benefit of the state? Caesar warned that all bad precedents originate in cases that were good. Caesar not only spoke this way; examine his conduct after he came to power.

He recalled in his speech the Lacedaemonians, who, when they conquered Athens, sent thirty men to govern them. These men began at first to put to death without trial the most wicked Greeks, and the Athenians rejoiced. But what started with the support of the Greeks spread, and afterwards the whole nation was reduced to slavery. He cited Sulla who ordered the proscriptions on profiteers and whose first executions were commended by all. But this was only the beginning of great bloodshed, and the massacre did not end until Sulla had glutted his followers with riches. Caesar said he did not fear the accused, but the possibility that when someone else is consul he will again draw his sword using as his precedent the execution of these men. He recommended that the goods of the prisoners be confiscated and they themselves be held in prison without possibility of appealing against the decision.

The Senate was almost convinced by Caesar when Cato, a man of the Stoic school, whose motto might be summed up in the phrase, "though the world collapse, let justice prevail," rose to speak. This, he contended, was a different situation. Let these men be liberals but not at the cost of our blood. The Roman used to feel that, you don't hurt me if you kill me, but you do if you reduce my status and let me live. Cato demanded that those who had confessed should be punished in the manner of their Roman forefathers. The decision was taken and the men were executed.

Sallust, in treating this period, manifests his friendship for Caesar by concealing Caesar's involvement with Cataline.

He recounts Cataline's remarks to his men, when he saw that he was beaten. Speaking to his soldiers, he told them that they were fighting for their country and for their life while their enemy was engaged in a futile contest to uphold the power of a few men. They might have passed their lives in exile, but they had all decided on this course. None save the victor desires peace. Cataline cautioned them to take care not to die unavenged, to leave the enemy a bloody and a tearful victory. In describing the event, Sallust betrays admiration for a man with whom he had no sympathy. He says that Cataline fell in the thick of the battle, and Sallust marvels at the boldness of Cataline's followers, all of whom died where they were stationed, from wounds inflicted from the front. Cataline's body was found later, far in advance of his men.

The Cataline group had no political status. They had created their own army. It had been possible to do this in Rome, since the main army was out of the country in the east. Under circumstances like these, the only way to get things done was by coercive power. The men who were now the malcontents in Cataline's army, in earlier days had had the threat of an external enemy as a prospect. What prospect did they have now? When there was fighting to be done, the men of Rome were necessary. There were other peoples about who could produce far better than the Romans. The Syrians were very talented; they made good doctors and teachers and they were good at writing. Unlike the Romans, they were good working men.

After the conspiracy of Cataline failed, Caesar knew

that because of his faint involvement in the affair, he was in jeopardy. He decided it would be better to leave Rome, and went to Spain. He had gotten into great debt to Crassus, but before he left he wanted to give one last party, so he borrowed more money from Crassus. Afterward he went to Spain to gather together some money in order to pay back his debt. Crassus could have easily become a leader when Pompey turned on the Senate. But instead the Senate turned against him, throwing him into Caesar's arms. Caesar, who knew how to spend money but not how to make it, needed his backing. In Spain he was a good governor, making much money without alienating the population.

Pompey returned and did an incredible thing which clearly showed that Sulla was still in the back of his mind. He disbanded his army, hoping that he would thereby get the support of the Senate. When the Senate realized there was no army with which it had to contend, it was overwhelmed by so much luck and lost its self-restraint. (Self-restraint is easier in the upper classes, but it is hard there, too.) It drove Pompey into the arms of Caesar.

Caesar returned from Spain and proposed to Pompey and Crassus that they stop contending with each other. Together, they could dominate Rome and no power could oppose them. Military prestige, money, and popular support — these were the big three. Out of their agreement to cooperate emerged the First Triumvirate. It was not a legal institution but an arrangement between the one who could move the masses, one who could buy anything, and one who had prestige. Caesar had the brains and boldness to control the crowd, Crassus had the money, and the front man who had dignity and influence with the middle class was Pompey.

Caesar was elected consul in 59 B.C. and decided to go to Gaul. The distribution of powers between triumvirate was to be overseen by Caesar. To bind this agreement, Caesar's daughter was given in marriage to Pompey. The founding of Rome, according to Roman tradition, came of the battle between two brothers, when the strongest fought it out. Events seemed to be conspiring to make certain that the next time two great bulls, Antony and Octavian, fought it out, they would be blood kin, just as in the beginning. It is awesome to consider how perfectly the cycle repeated itself.

The command Caesar gave himself was very important. He was about forty years old then, and gave himself his first real military command. Until his command in Gaul, Caesar worked exclusively as a demagogue. But after observing the Cataline incident, and the lack of restraint of the Senate in its relation to Pompey when he had no army, and the even greater lack of restraint of the starved populace, each group making endless demands of the other, Caesar must have wondered what it would take to satisfy everyone's demands.

What did Caesar lack? He lacked an army that knew him as its master. There is no question that he knew Rome would be divided against itself. During this strife she would have to be protected. Caesar went into Germany to prevent the Germans from coming into Rome someday. He convinced the Germans so well that they remained convinced for 400 years. If the Germans had taken Gaul, the history of Europe would have been different.

Bear in mind what Polybius had prophesied would happen to Rome. The emergence of individuals during this period has distracted historians from the simplicity of the development. After the enemy, Carthage, had been removed, many people began to suggest plans about what should be done with the energy and money that had been released from the necessity of defending Rome. When there is great wealth and no external enemy to channel its expenditure, many people will arise with suggestions as to what should be done with this wealth. This is how, during this period, so very many personalities emerged. When a people has an enemy, they are unselfish. When the enemy ceases to exist, they become selfish and try to make their selfishness appear unselfish. Men stepped forward now and proclaimed what they stood for. They were men with plans. And this is what the personalities of this period mean. Every whim of a positive goal could lead a man to fame if he could only back his whim with money and rhetoric. If all these personalities are pushed aside, however, Polybius becomes the best guide for this period.

To understand the meaning of Augustus, one must understand the mixed constitution of Polybius and the dynamics of revolution as formulated by Plato and Aristotle.

We have indicated that Sulla intended to restore the mixed constitution. He had tried to restore the power of the three elements of this constitution. Sulla had actually tried to give power back to them, and the result was chaos. These three elements became involved in the civil wars. Basically, it was these three interests that met in the first Triumvirate. The problem posed was, were these interests to remain in a condition of civil war? Would not one strong power keep them in line? A man would have to somehow take the power away from these three elements and then give it back to them, and they would have to willingly return it to him. To avoid tyranny, the power of a Sulla was needed. But the three interests had to return it to Sulla willingly. But would you still have a republic? What would happen if they refused to return it? There would be a re-run of all the events that followed from Pompey to Actium. Augustus achieved the power of a Sulla, and he returned it to the three interests, but if they had kept it they could only have looked forward to civil wars.

Polybius, when he looked at the Republican constitution of Rome, asked who it was that ruled in Rome. Was it the consuls, the senate, or the people? Who was it that enforced the law? This is the charm of a mixed constitution; nobody has the highest power to enforce the law.

The three elements of the constitution had a distribution of power, but the force behind the three was the enemy. It was the enemy who reminded these elements not to try to usurp one another's power, thereby weakening the republic. For should they have done so, the enemy would have stepped in. During this period, the Romans had bloodless class strife. In Athens a class protest would have meant bloodshed every time.

Political freedom means not having a specific body that enforces the law.

Montesquieu points out that wherever there is not a mixed constitution, there is a concentration of power in one group, which becomes the source of the law and the means of its enforcement. Otherwise the nation is an easy prey to its enemies. Freedom means the separation of this power. He points out that even in the Venetian Republic of the Renaissance, there was no freedom because the three powers were concentrated in one. This concentration of power is painful to bear when the state is strong enough to survive without it. There are two times when an Augustus is needed. One of these is when a country is too weak to defeat an enemy, even if it is united.

If the conduct of affairs were left to the party system in France, or the little nations of South America, nothing would ever get done. There is here a necessity for one-man rule, as the enemy is too strong to be coped with even by a united nation. The other time an Augustus is needed occurred only in Rome. This was when no enemy was strong enough to make them unite.

Polybius wrote after the second Punic War before the final destruction of Carthage. Yet he foresaw the pattern of events that would inevitably lead to an Augustus. He writes:

> Some seek to become more powerful than the ordinary citizens; and the most liable to this temptation are the rich. So when they begin to be fond of office, and find themselves unable to obtain it by their own unassisted efforts and their own merits, they ruin their estates, while enticing and corrupting the common people in

every possible way. By which means, when in their senseless mania for reputation they have made the populace ready and greedy to receive bribes, the virtue of democracy is destroyed, and it is transformed into a government of violence and the strong hand. For the mob, habituated to feed at the expense of others, and to have its hopes of a livelihood in the property of its neighbors, as soon as it has got a leader sufficiently ambitious and daring, being excluded by poverty from the sweets of civil honors, produces a reign of mere violence. Then come tumultuous assemblies, massacres, banishments, redivisions of land; until after losing all trace of civilization, it has once more found a master and a despot. (VI, 9)

This was written before Cataline and the rebellious slaves, before the marvelous moment of Gracchian idealism after which the people became greedy. At the end of this process, Polybius predicts a master and despot.[27]

The situation under which the despot arrived can be compared to what Polybius said we see happen in the case of animals that are without the faculty of reason, such as bulls, goats, and cocks, among whom there can be no dispute that the strongest take the lead. It was a situation where, as with the animals, there would be a struggle among the natural leaders to determine who would lead. There were the great bulls: Caesar, eager to increase his power; Crassus, eager to acquire distinction; and Pompey, who in dignity and influence towered above them both. Caesar went to Gaul, Crassus to Asia, Pompey to Spain. With their three vast armies, they held the empire of the world. The First Triumvirate takes us back to the way the Roman state began, when Romulus united three tribes, which were probably Caesar-like, Crassus-like and Pompey-like. This representation of three interests is always present, united by external force. It is almost miraculous to watch these three appear. Why three? Why not two? It is a natural process with Rome. This is the way Rome grew. Lycurgus had done it in Sparta deliberately. Pompey and Caesar were relatives just as were Romulus and Remus, and after Caesar's daughter (who had been Pompey's wife) died, Caesar and Pompey eyed each other with mutual envy.

They were not consciously acting according to the pattern of Polybius, and yet events fell out that way. Appian describes that event so reminiscent of Romulus and Remus, so completely fratricidal, when these two leaders locked horns at the battle of Pharsalus, contending for supremacy.

Pompey gave the first signal for that battle which marked the end of the republic, on a battlefield as chaotic as Polybius could ask. Out of the chaos came unity. Caesar sent heralds with the message to spare the Romans on the opposing side, to slay only the auxiliaries. Caesar gained to his side all the companions of Pompey. He had not been fighting a war against Pompey's supporters, only against Pompey. And the people were beginning to realize their need for one ruler.

Augustus was to do the same thing. But Caesar was a preliminary run-through. He was more Sulla-like in his intentions. As a consequence of his amnesty, Caesar was proclaimed father of his country, dictator for life, and was deified. The wearied people hoped he would restore the Republic to them as Sulla had done. But Caesar disappointed them. It was not the right time to give back his rule. It required a beneficent gesture first. Before the rule is returned, something obviously necessary must be gradually withdrawn. Caesar had a powerful personal guard; he dismissed them and walked about Rome alone.

Appian describes the assassination of Caesar, where Cassius drove the dagger first and Caesar fought with rage and outcries like a wild animal, hurling Cassius back with violence, until he was stabbed by Brutus; then he covered his face and slid to the ground. After he had fallen, 23 wounds were inflicted by the conspirators.

This is not the Caesar of Shakespeare, who could not treat Caesar with sympathy, since he had to reserve this for Brutus. Only in this way could he develop his play to its soul-shaking conclusion when Brutus realizes that Caesar was right. This is why, though the play is largely about Brutus, it is called *Julius Caesar*, for he dominates it throughout and at the end.

Before Caesar and Pompey, there had been lesser animals fighting it out, cocks like Cicero and Cataline. And after these bulls would come another set of animals to fight it out on an even greater stage.

The reason Augustus got the support of Italy was because, unlike Caesar, he was not democratic. He realized the tremendous desire to be equal, but he was not anxious to make everybody equal. By favoring the Italic people, Augustus almost generated a national feeling.

The most interesting aspect of Roman history is the achievement of Augustus. Rostovtzeff refers to the difficulties of determining what his achievement was, pointing out that the best one can say is that no one thing happened. Tacitus describes the achievement of Augustus in this manner:

> When after the destruction of Brutus and Cassius there was no longer any army of the commonwealth, when Pompeus was crushed in Sicily, and when, with Lepidus pushed aside and Antonius slain, even the Julian faction had only Caesar left to lead it, then, dropping the title of Triumvir, and giving out that he was a Consul, and was satisfied with a tribune's authority for the protection of the people, Augustus won over the soldiers with gifts, the populace with cheap grain, and all men with the sweets of repose, and so grew greater by degrees, while he concentrated in himself the functions of the senate, the magistrates, and the laws.

Tacitus here describes the achievement of Augustus in one sentence, and nothing has ever been written about Augustus that says more than this. Augustus had kept the semblance of the form of the republic while concentrating all power into his own hands and lulling all men into repose. We should remember that Tacitus was a Republican, and was not interested in repose but in the alertness that is the price of freedom. He goes on to say:

> He was wholly unopposed, for the boldest spirits had fallen in battle, or in the proscription, while the remaining nobles, the readier they were to be slaves, were raised the higher by wealth and promotion, so that, aggrandized by revolution, they preferred the safety of the present to the dangerous past.

The bold spirits that Tacitus refers to were the nobility who Polybius had said would rise up against tyranny and whom he tried to imbue with the means for delaying the devolution of power.

Tacitus continues:

> Nor did the provinces dislike that condition of affairs, for they distrusted the government of the senate and the people, because of the rivalries between the leading men and the rapacity of the officials, while the protection of the laws was unavailing, as they were continually deranged by violence, intrigue, and finally by corruption.

What, after all, could be wrong with having an Augustus? If there were five hundred ambitious powerful men in Rome, Rome had five hundred oppressors. If there were only one powerful man, there would be only one oppressor. How much better could the situation be? But the Roman people found it difficult to trust the power of this one office to any man. They wanted to examine the credentials of the man first, before creating the office. They had had such a man in Julius Caesar, but they did not like him. They killed him. They thought that thereby they would restore the freedom of the old republic. They restored, instead, bloody civil wars. Eventually the Romans learned that the office must precede the man, that the means must first be provided before a man could fulfill the function of this office. Some bad men, it is true, did assume this power. But this was no serious obstacle to the efficiency of the office, for there was, as Hegel points out, a remedy for a bad emperor: death.

The plan was to bring peace to Rome by concentrating sufficient power in one man, in office, so that there would be no danger of overthrowing it. There were two possible forms of military power on which this office might be based.

Caesar experimented with one of the possible forms. He was an absolute equalitarian; he had a divine attitude. He treated his friends and his enemies alike, distinctions did not matter, and he planned to derive his military legions from the entire empire. He offended the noble people who, since they were called upon to sacrifice their power to Caesar, wanted to be credited proportionately for their sacrifice. If two men are called upon to sacrifice their weapons, the man turning in a cannon might feel that he should get more credit for his sacrifice than the man who had turned in a bean-shooter. He might insist that there should be some status attached to sacrifice. But Caesar was like Gulliver looking down upon the Lilliputians. Among the Lilliputians a man who was considered awesome in stature by his fellows was in reality only a hair's breadth taller than they, and Gulliver from his height could perceive no difference. It did not matter to Caesar whether he was dealing with friends or enemies, all were equally disarmed, and all received equal recognition.

Anthony was the correct heir to Caesar's power. He had fought on Caesar's side and shared his ideas. He saw that it was possible to rule Rome from Egypt or from any point in the empire. When Caesar was in Gaul, he ruled Rome from Gaul. Where Caesar was, there was the center of the Empire. This was the secret that Anthony had in mind which later emperors were to find out. But it is not good to divulge a secret prematurely.

It was this secret, when revealed, that enabled Augustus to take Rome and the people and the senate. He employed the second form of military power based on the people of Rome, who were Italians and inhabited the

Italian peninsula. He favored the disgruntled nobles, the best men, the best fighters, that Caesar had ignored, and they gave him just that decisive balance of power which he needed to defeat Anthony. After the battle was over, Augustus gave this power, which he had gotten through Civil War, back to the people. He was not anything other than an heir to an army as Sulla had been, and as Sulla had done, he too returned his power.

But the senate and the people of Rome knew what they owed him, and we have it in so many words from the people and senate. What kind of power was it that the people of Rome returned to Augustus? It was the ultimate coercive power in the state.

Before the destruction of Carthage, as Sullust had rightly observed, the ultimate coercive power had been outside of Rome in the shape of the enemy.

What Augustus achieved is expressed by the Code of Justinian in two maxims. The first maxim is *quod principe placuit legis habet vigorem*, which means that whatever pleases the first officer has the force of law.[28]

Taken abstractly, this power which to the Roman was centered in the *princips* could in different situations be implicit elsewhere. The power of the *princips* could be our majority rule, or it could be senatorial power, or the faction in power. But the Justinian Code observes that although the principle gives the force of law to the pleasure of the first officer, of itself it is not legal. How is it made legal? By the *Lex Regia*, which is the conferring of this imperial power on the office of the *princips* by the people of Rome. Before the fall of Carthage, the people had never had this much power to confer. But after the destruction of Carthage and the lesser enemies of Rome, all these vanquished forces embodied in the returning victorious Roman legions were drawn back and focused at Rome. In order to bring peace to Rome, the enemy had to be reconstituted. It had to be stronger than Carthage ever was.

This new external enemy that surpassed the combined strength of all the factions in Rome was the only thing that could hold the Roman people together. Sulla had achieved this power and he gave Rome one more chance at freedom by returning it. But he knew that without it the Roman factions would cut each other to pieces, and he prophesied that no man after him having achieved this power again would dare to willingly lay it aside.

The second maxim, *princeps legibus solutus*, means that the first officer, though his pleasure is law and he alone can enforce the law, is not bound by it. If the *princeps* were as vulnerable to his law as his subjects, then he would not be external to them, nor would he be supreme.[29] The power that is here described is possible as a law only when a state has no enemy. It cannot be taken as a general legal principle.

The achievement of Augustus was the expression of Roman Natural Law. It was the culmination of rational law in the Roman experience. The application of reason to Roman law took 150 years. The basis for it had been evolving for many centuries.

Cicero wrote of the law that transcends law, but he also asked if a state had the right to legislate itself out of existence. He concluded that it did not. Were the United States Congress to decide to pass a law submitting its sovereignty to another power, it would at that instant lose its authority to pass that law, by violating the very authority which the people had given it to legislate for them. During this hypothetical self-imposed legal vacuum, the law of the land could rightfully be determined by whoever was strong enough to stave off the enemy that might try to step in to claim sovereignty.

The safety of a nation is the highest law. In order to have law at all, there must be a nation, a body politic. Just as to have a law of falling bodies there must be falling bodies. Law cannot legally undo its subject, the basis which called it into being. The preservation of the body politic, without which there could be no law, is the highest law.

Rome had reached a condition where she had no competition; there was no external enemy. The legal dilemma arose. How, without an external enemy to enforce her laws for her, was she to enforce obedience to her own laws? It is nice to be able to get the willing support of the law infractor. The crime and its punishment are defined. The situation is set up in advance. The act has a built-in remedy. The crime and the punishment are one continuous act. Through civil strife Roman society had selected the laws it needed.

But the ultimate law that required a complete scaling of all the laws of nations and was the rationalization of the whole body of law, that eliminated civil laws and foreign laws—that was the achievement of Augustus, the *digno vox*. Rome set up a Medusa's head. But the Romans expected the emperor to obey his own laws even though they could not force him to do so.

The principate inaugurated by Augustus is the only form of government that is easily defined. When the Greco-Roman world learned the meaning of the *digno vox*, the Medusa's head of laws, it became very sad. It learned that freedom equals war and peace equals a prison house. Once the secret is known, the Greco-Roman world dies. On this subject, Hegel writes:

> The first thing to be remarked respecting the imperial rule is that the Roman government was so abstracted from interest that the great transition to that rule hardly changed anything in the constitution. [By abstracted from interest, Hegel means that it had no particular thing that it wanted to do, since all it had to do was to gain the power to do whatever it wanted.] The popular assemblies alone were unsuited to the new state of things, and disappeared. The emperor was *princeps senatus*, censor, consul, tribune; he united all their nominally continuing offices in himself; and the military

power—here the most essentially important—was exclusively in his hands. The constitution was an utterly insubstantial form, from which all vitality, consequently all might and power, had departed; and the only means of maintaining its existence were the legions which the emperor constantly kept in the vicinity of Rome. Public business was indeed brought before the senate, and the emperor appeared simply as one of its members; but the senate was obliged to obey, and whoever ventured to gainsay his will was punished with death, and his property confiscated. Those, therefore, who had certain death in anticipation, killed themselves, that if they could do nothing more, they might at least preserve their property to their family. (*Philosophy of History*, 314)

Rostovtzeff wonders what Augustus would have done, had the Romans refused to return his power to him. The situation was quite simple. Augustus had all the power, an army absolutely committed to him, but he did not have the consent of the people. So, with an absolutely committed army looking on, an army that would have followed no one but him, he gave the army to the senators. It must have occurred to the uneasy senators that although the gift was magnanimous, it would be dreadful if Augustus was bluffing. They took the intelligent course by immediately returning the army to Augustus. Tacitus was later to observe that he believed Augustus was faking. Be that as it may, Augustus could now say that he had given the army to the Senate and they had returned it. And whereas before he had had all the power without the consent of the people, he now had all the power with the consent of the people.

The Romans must have grasped the necessity of an Augustus. This is another illustration of the Hegelian observation that that which is necessary in history, though it may be rejected by the people the first time, will be accepted the second. The Romans thought that Julius Caesar had done something unnecessary, so they killed him. They then discovered it was necessary after all. The party that had opposed Caesar paved the way for two heads instead of one, and these had to fight it out again. The second time around, Augustus asked: "Have you learned yet?" This time he got the people's consent. The Romans had killed Caesar but accepted Augustus. Although in later years they were to kill many unsuitable emperors, it never crossed their minds to restore the republic. What was the republic but six armies trying to kill each other?

Rostovtzeff maintains that there is no simple definition for the achievement of Augustus, yet he says:

> When Augustus had defeated Antony, his power rested upon his sole command over the armed forces of the state. [What is this but the first maxim, *quod principe placuit*?]

Rostovtzeff continues:

> When he laid down his extraordinary powers in 27 B.C., he abdicated also his command over the army . . . his military power was immediately handed back to him by the Senate. [Here we have *Lex Regia*.] How he would have acted if the Senate had not done this, we do not know [*digno vox*]. It did confer on him proconsular power for ten years in all the provinces where armies were quartered, except Africa and Macedonia. But it is notable that the senate made no attempt to take this power from him: his connection with the army was too close to be dissolved by any decree they could pass [*princeps legibus solutus* — the first officer is not bound by the law.] (*Rome*, 167)

These maxims were perused by the medieval legalists at Bologna and formed the essential basis of the power of the medieval emperors. These maxims also made the Greeks and Romans listen to the Jews.

The Romans were the only people who went so far in their legal experience as to be almost hyperlegal, by defining the maxims underlying the principate. The "prerogative powers" of England are a comparable instance. These powers have been deliberately left undefined by

British legalists. Their very definition would result, according to Maitland, in a political paralysis. Every investigation into the nature of sovereignty inevitably leads to a popular paralysis. The ultimate source of sovereignty is not defined unless it absolutely cannot be concealed. The Romans were the only people who had reached a point where it could not be concealed.

The closest approach to a definition of sovereignty in American history was the Civil War. Lincoln, in order to preserve the constitution, had to violate the constitution. The Hegelian understands this, since he realizes that there is always, essentially, in everything, the negative moment. Thomas Jefferson has expressed the view that a strict observance of laws is not the highest law. A strict adherence to the written law might in some cases involve losing the law itself, by undermining the survival of the country. Jefferson points out that when the safety of the nation is at stake, the good officer may have to decide to act outside the laws of his nation in order to preserve the nation. He does this at his own peril, for his extra-constitutional acts are an illegal gamble. If they are miscalculations, then he must be prepared to die after. Robespierre and Cromwell were well-meaning officers of the state who decided to take extra-legal measures to preserve the state.

Lincoln, in his correspondence, explained his actions with respect to slavery. He personally deprecated slavery, but he considered this to be his own abstract judgment and did not permit it to interfere with his larger concern, which was to uphold his oath to preserve the union. Was it desirable, he asked, to uphold the Constitution at the cost of losing the union? The measures he took, he freely admitted, were unconstitutional, but they were seen by him as essential to preserve the union, and he held out hope that they might subsequently become lawful if it were necessary thereby to preserve the Constitution. The destruction of Carthage meant that the Romans had to face a situation comparable to the one Lincoln faced, not once in their history, but every day. What happened after the fall of Carthage, in Rome, when she faced a national emergency every single day, when crisis was a permanent situation? She had to develop an ever-present non-constitutional power to preserve the constitution.[30] Rome created a built-in enemy that did what Lincoln said had to be done in a crisis. It acted unconstitutionally to preserve the constitution. But whereas in other nations such a crisis would emerge rarely, in Rome it was ever-present and consequently so was the built-in enemy.

The only Roman law that survives actively in the world today is the third phase of Roman law, Natural Law. This alone can be adapted and used by a modern nation. It would certainly be senseless to use the *ius civile* or *ius gentium*, since modern nations have evolved their own civil laws. The Roman law that lives today is not the law under which Rome's influence expanded over Italy, nor the law under which she took the Mediterranean World, but the law a state must use after conquering the enemy which it needs to hold itself together. The Natural Law of Rome alone is adaptable to the modern world, but it can be used by a nation without absurdity only when it has no external enemies. Natural Law was so well wrought that even after the Romans stopped enforcing it; it enforced itself. It survived Roman power. The Germans who overwhelmed Rome were awed by the majesty of her law. German power displaced Roman power, but Roman law and order was retained. The power of the Germans was combined with the law of the Romans. Roman law survives throughout most of Europe and in America today.

The greatest disaster of modern times was the introduction of the Roman Natural Law into the jurisprudence of European nations.[31]

Of the spirit of the Augustan age Rostovtzeff observes:

After the horrors of civil war, the idea of civic freedom

— an idea closely connected by the Romans with the idea of the state — had become, in the minds of most men, inseparable from the anarchy and confusion which were still so fresh in the memory of the generation contemporary with Augustus. (*Rome*, 183)

With Augustus Rome achieved peace but lost its freedom. After one hundred years of bloody civil wars, everyone was reconciled to the enforcement of peace, but it saddened them. The literature of the time breathed sadness. It is hard to detect in it Epicurean writing. But when it became sophisticated, it betrayed this sadness, a sadness which might be described as boredom intensified by tremendous longing, a condition of mind without remedy comparable to the state of a man who has all the appetites and is in a position to have anything he likes, and yet somehow finds it all meaningless (*la dolce vita*). Some literary people acquire this disposition of boredom without even having troubled to enjoy life's pleasures. The despondency of Rome after Augustus should be compared to the despondency of the Hellenistic Greeks after Alexander.

The ideal of the Greeks had been that the wise man merged with the necessary instrument of happiness, the state. But when the possibility of the self-sufficient Greek state had been removed, the Greek ideal became the wise man who found happiness in himself alone. The pursuit of happiness became internal. It took the three forms of epicureanism, stoicism, and skepticism, with a later tendency toward eclecticism.

Before the destruction of Carthage, an effort had been made by Polybius and Panaetius to socialize Greek Stoic doctrine again, by applying Greek thought to a class, instead of to individuals, the other two classes being restrained by the constant presence of an external enemy. The crowning achievement of the Greek wise man had been the suggestion that those who have power should not abuse it, the admonition that all the power in the state should not be concentrated in one group.

The Romans were to learn that it is impossible to have one self-restraining class without an enemy, for it is the presence of an enemy that gives force to the words of that class. When the enemy was gone, the Romans were to find that they had to create an internal equivalent to the enemy's force, and the knowledge of this made Rome despondent.

But despondency can also be beautiful. There is a beauty in sadness. Those who fail to perceive this have never enjoyed the pleasure of the sentimental existence. There is enjoyment in facing the pessimism and despondency of life, in drowning one's self in the sweet realization that the universe is chaos and that the grandest thing about man is that he is able to face the fact that he is nothing. This realization produced very beautiful literature.

Of the Roman writers, many people today prefer Catullus because he was an aristocrat and most literary people are aristocratic in spirit. Rostovtzeff says:

> The Augustan age produced worthy rivals of Cicero and Catullus. Most conspicuous is the group of great poets connected with Augustus through Gaius Maecenas, a passionate lover of literature and art, and the emperor's friend and minister. This group, which was adorned by the names of Virgil and Horace, it is the custom to describe as a group of court poets, whose business was to glorify Augustus. Most of them had been ruined by the revolution and depended for support upon Augustus and his intimate friends. But it is not likely that Augustus forced them to accept his views. They did not owe it to his patronage that they were recognized as classics in their own lifetime by all who spoke the Latin language. In this matter also, Augustus showed his knowledge of human nature and his sensitiveness to prevalent feeling. He knew that Virgil and Horace could not help writing in his favor; he felt that their genius would express in a succession of unforgettable images the fundamental ideas of his reign. It is impossible that the burning words

which we read on many pages of the *Aeneid* were suggested to Virgil by Augustus: they poured forth from the poet's own heart, and they found sympathetic and enthusiastic hearers and readers, not only in Augustus and his family, but among Romans everywhere. (*Rome*, 190-191)

The poetry of Virgil has had a far more tremendous influence in the western world than that of Homer. The Romans were the last people who truly understood Homer. The learned Romans were conversant in Greek in a way that some modern scholars are in Latin, and they could still recapture the greatness of Homer, which could not be translated from Greek into another language. To the modern scholar only that greatness of Homer survives which is translatable.

Virgil dominated all Roman literature which was produced after him as well as the literature of the Middle Ages. He had a powerful influence on Dante, who called Virgil his master. The highest achievement of Virgil was his capacity to make poetry out of poetry. Virgil in the *Aeneid* wrote the greatest imitative poem.

One should distinguish between original poetry and imitative poetry. Original poetry does not require a literary education, a cultivated audience, or a good memory, that is, a familiarity with earlier works. Its greatness lies in the words of the poem itself.

In this respect Homer was an original poet. No one knows how dependent Homer was on preceding poets, and it is certain that he used the material of earlier poets for his work, but it is also certain that there was no greater poet before Homer. Originality consists in the ability of arranging commonplace words with commonplace significance in such a way as to give them a newness wherein they acquire that infinite suggestiveness which is the mark of poetry. Shakespeare excels in this talent. What, for instance, could be plainer and yet more suggestive than his phrase, "the rest is silence." Homer also excelled in this talent.

Imitative or literary poetry, on the other hand, sends countless echoes through the mind that has a literary education and is familiar with earlier works. The greatest imitative or literary poet in the English language was Milton.

Dante was capable of both kinds of poetry. Part of Dante's talent consisted in his ability to take ordinary words and arrange them in such a way as to give them striking suggestiveness. Intrinsically the arrangement of the words need not mean anything specific, but it imparts the feeling that there is a meaning even if it is not plain what the meaning is. Dante's phrase, "in my beautiful St. John," of itself does not mean a thing and yet unfailingly brings tears to Italian eyes whenever Dante is read and that phrase is reached. But the other part of Dante's talent was his tremendous capacity to take old poetry and make it like new. Virgil guides Dante through the *Inferno* and takes him to the top of purgatory, but then Virgil is dismissed and Dante's girlfriend enters. It was characteristic of the Romans to use the color white for the triumph and for death. "Give lilies with full hands." This was the passage which brought tears to the wife of Augustus Caesar and inclined her to have Augustus endow Virgil. When Dante sees his girl appear, the angels sing "strew lilies." For anyone who knows Virgil, it is apparent that the lilies are not only for Beatrice but also for Virgil. Just as Dante sees Beatrice, Virgil disappears. His master was gone,

The great advantage Virgil had over Homer was that he was the poet of a vast state. It is much easier for such a poet to make grand statements. Contrast Shakespeare to D'Annunzio. The grand statements of the latter fall flat, whereas the Britannia of Shakespeare ruled the waves. When the glory of a nation descends, it is not so easy for its poets to write great poetry. Shakespeare, it is well to remember, was writing in the glorious days after the defeat of the Spanish Armada.

In Virgil, we find a poetic summary of the history of

Rome which as it progresses becomes sadder and sadder. It is the saddest poem of praise ever written. Aeneas, the hero of Virgil, unlike the Homeric heroes who were beyond good and evil, is pious and concerned to do his duty. The only reason he had been allowed to escape from Troy was that he might found a new Troy. While on his way to carry out this mission, he gets sidetracked by a storm to North Africa, where the queen, Dido, forces him to tell her about Troy and falls in love with him. Aeneas is almost tempted to settle down, but the gods remind him why he was permitted to escape from Troy, and that he must therefore go on. He makes preparations to leave secretly, while Dido, enraged at his having taken her love and rejected it, puts a curse on him and all his descendants, condemning his people and hers to eternal warfare. It is tender to think that this imperial period could produce such a poetic explanation of the Carthaginian wars, and such an apology for the treatment by pious Aeneas of Dido, who was worthy of better treatment.

There was a tendency expressed in Virgil and the epicureans and the mystic writers, to turn back to a Golden Age. Anything seemed preferable to the awful boredom and longing of the present. Even civil war would be better than this depression and despondency. There would not be time to get bored. But the present was dominated by that great equalizing imperial steamroller which kept rolling back and forth over men's heads, flattening them into such perfect equality that they would later have to be propped up with force in order to get them to do anything. The Roman poets sang about olden times. The voices the Romans wanted to hear were those of the past, of the ancient writers of the days when men were close to divinity. The magic name of Pythagoras came to be used freely, and many sayings acquired authority because they were attributed to him. What did these men of the past have? They had spontaneous open hearts; they were closer to divinity.

The writers of Rome became prophets, quoting the

sayings of the past. The Roman felt he could come closer to the gods by reading them. The Roman was urged to give up pride and reason. He began to look forward to a new golden age. The Roman could look back and say he had done all that was possible.

Was it not the Greeks who discovered that man's nature was driven by the two horses, Thymos and Epithemia, the noble spirited part and the avaricious appetitive part? Did they not say that the horses must be restrained so that *Nous*, reason, could develop? Was not justice to them the balance of the virtues of courage, temperance and prudence? Had not Plato said that this balance of virtues was possible only within the state? But when the Greeks lost the state, the cult of wise men sought happiness within themselves, and their doctrine fell into the contradiction of holding that this happiness could be achieved without the state.

The Roman had revived the insight that the highest law was the survival of the state and pursued it through civil wars until he had created a power that was strong enough to enable the state to survive. It was perfectly possible to kill the man who wielded this power, but the power itself must remain to draw the desire for strife out of the Romans. (And to ultimately give occasion for many hundreds of later historians to write books, pondering the question of why Rome fell.) Rome fell from love of peace. Not from any real enemies, just those smart enough not to love peace.

All the human means devised during Greco-Roman history had been employed by the Romans to arrive at a state of tremendous despondency and longing in the Age of Augustus.

Was it conceivable to have done all this and thereby come to nothing? The nothingness of the present turned the Roman to looking for authority in the past and to revelation for salvation in the future. Men arose to remind the Romans that there had lived men in other times who knew how to live in the present (Buddha, Zoroaster). Zen Buddhism became very popular in Rome, no less than it is today in the United States.

Bertrand Russell in an essay of 1902 asked what it was that was behind the spirit of the Englishman and the American. On what should we found the brotherhood of man? He came to the very moving conclusion that we should found it on "nothing." Matthew Arnold has expressed this view in poetry.

> Ah love, let us be true
> To one another! for the world, which seems
> To lie before us like a land of dreams,
> So various, so beautiful, so new,
> Hath really neither joy nor love, nor light,
> Nor certitude, nor peace, nor help for pain;
> And we are here as on a darkling plain,
> Swept with alarms of struggle and flight,
> Where ignorant armies clash by night.

Arnold says, "Ah love, let us be true/To one another!" What reason does he give? Only that there is no such thing as love.

The spirit of the Romans is not so far removed from us. The modern man, as the sale of paperback books will attest, feels much closer in spirit to the twilight of Virgil than to the dawn of Homer.

IV. THE THIRD PHASE
THE EMPIRE AFTER THE DEATH OF AUGUSTUS

Rostovtzeff says of Tacitus:

> His penetration into the minds of the different rulers and those who stood round the throne is profound. If any one wishes to learn the characters of the immediate successors of Augustus, he may and must read what remains of [the *Annals* and the *Histories*]. All that has been written later about this period by ancient or modern historians is either a faint reflection of his genius or dry and lifeless extracts from his writings. (*Rome*, 194)

There is so little to say about the politics of the Roman Empire. About all that one can do is to give the names and behavior of the emperors. Tacitus complained about the history he was writing, which he ruefully observed was largely an inquiry into whether the emperor's wife was faithful.

The biggest issue over which to fight a war during this period was the enforcement of peace, which in effect meant everyone was to stay where they were, and if they were to get ahead, they were to get ahead evenly. It is interesting to compare Tacitus' complaint about the subject matter of Roman history with the complaint of the Emperor Caligula who lamented that nothing was going on in the Roman Empire.

Caligula looked back wistfully at the old timers of Roman history and yearned for the wonderful opportunities they had to do revolutionary deeds. Surrounded by enemies, they had built up the Roman state.

What happened politically during this period was very simple. What happens in any revolution? A revolution must accomplish three things.

First, it must set up the principle for which it is being fought, such as the banner, "Liberty, Equality, Fraternity," of the French Revolution. Second, after the principle is established, it must set up the institution by which it is to be carried out. Third, it must create a popular disposition to support the principle that has been institutionalized.

Julius Caesar knew the principle, which was that there must be one ruler, and all his subjects must be equal. But, though he established the principle, he did not succeed in carrying it out.

Sulla, though he was unaware of the principle, had earlier developed the institution whereby it was to be carried out. This was by complete concentration of power.

It was left for Augustus to combine the principle and the institution. The first principle of the Romans was to establish that everyone was equal under the principate. But it was not easy to get the popular disposition to accept this principle.

Augustus defeated Anthony precisely because Anthony had tried to carry out Caesar's principle prematurely. The ultimate goal, however, was to achieve the acceptance of the principle.

The emperors after Augustus variously worked toward this end. The immediate successor of Augustus, Tiberius, was a rough, tough soldier in the old tradition, who did not contribute much to the new spirit. The man who made a really big contribution was Claudius. Although his mother and sister did not think much of him, the soldiers forced him to be emperor.

There came a time when the seats of the Senate had to be filled up and Claudius proposed they be taken by Gauls. His proposal was met with vehement Roman opposition. What distinctions would be left to the Romans if these millionaires, whose ancestors had destroyed Roman armies with fire and sword, were to be given such high honors? The opposition allowed them to enjoy the title of citizens, but not of senators. The reply of Claudius was worthy of Franklin Delano Roosevelt. He said that one must take all conspicuous merit wherever it is found. The fall of Athens and Sparta, he reminded his opposition, stemmed from the way these Greek states had spurned their enemies. He observed that what he was proposing was not so terrible but rather a common practice. Had not Rome enjoyed peace, united with the Gauls? Would it not be better to let the Gauls bring their gold to Rome, rather than to force them to enjoy it in isolation? Had not this process gone on throughout Roman history? Had not these rights been granted to the plebeians by the patricians, and later to the Latins, and later to other peoples? What he was proposing, Claudius maintained, was justified by precedent, and would itself become a precedent.

After Claudius came Nero, the last of the Augustan line, and then came that strange moment in Roman history, the year of the four emperors. The emperors that succeeded Augustus had been uneasy in office; they did not know how to justify their holding the supreme power. They did not yet know the secret and neither did the populace. But now during the year of the four emperors the secret came out. As Tacitus observes:

> Welcome as the death of Nero had been in the first burst of joy, yet it had not only roused various emotions in Rome, among the Senators, the people or the soldiery of the capital, it had also excited all the legions and their generals, for now had been divulged that secret of the empire, that emperors could be made elsewhere than at Rome.

The man who was emperor was unimportant. The purpose of that imperial steamroller to roll out the differences remained, regardless of who filled the office. The function of the emperor was abstracted and the person of the emperor could be derived from anywhere in the empire.

The year of the four emperors (69 A.D.) was a year of struggle in which three emperors passed in rapid succession and the fourth, Vespasian, established a new line, which concentrated on further extending the leveling process.

Hadrian was not Roman. He was one of the high ranking officers in the army. He pushed this process still further. As emperor he traveled about his empire to study economic conditions. He stayed out of Italy so long that he set up judges who ran Italy like a province. He diminished Italy but he adorned the whole Roman Empire with cities and monuments.

He was followed by the famous Septimus Severus, who went still further; and the culmination of the policy of Hadrian and Severus came in Caracalla when, in 211 B.C., he made every subject of the Roman Empire a citizen. (The laws of 88 B.C. were extended.)

During this period Rome had materially reached an apex. She enjoyed more general prosperity than any nation had, either before or after. She had maintained the externals of prosperity without the struggle which accompanies freedom.

The conquest of the Greco-Roman world by Christianity is important because it created a mirror image of the Roman empire without its political substance. There is a perfect parallel between the concept of the Roman Empire and the Judaic-Christian church.

The conquest of the Greco-Roman world by Judaic religion was as important as the rationalistic and legalistic achievement of Greece and Rome. These are the three great roots of the modern western world: Greek rationalism which is freedom, the freedom which the philosophers called insight into necessity; Roman law; and Jewish religion.

All peoples make, behave and explain. Yet it is almost miraculous to see how, among the three great peoples of antiquity, one of these activities always dominated the other two. The culmination of the Greek achievement was explaining; making and behaving were subordinated to it.

The culmination of the Roman achievement was making; explaining and behaving were subordinated to it. Roman making was done on the grandest scale: the making of the laws of a vast empire and of the great cities of the Greco-Roman world.

The culmination of the Jewish achievement was behaving; explaining and making were subordinated to a preoccupation with the principles of human behavior.

It was in the cities, under the aegis of Rome, principally Alexandria, that the height of intellectual activity was reached, not in the activity of a few isolated personalities as in Hellenic Greece, but in the cumulative influx and meeting of thought from all parts of the world which stimulated thinking of every kind. It was here that antiquity produced its only development that can be compared to modern science. We are in an age very similar to the one that produced Ptolemy and Archimedes, when men devoted themselves to that knowledge which lends itself to mathematical formulation.

The behavioral emphasis of the Jews was to overcome a world that had concentrated on explaining and making. The Greco-Roman world ends because of the Jews; it becomes a hangover after the Judaic conquest of Rome.

The Jews in connection with the east are insignificant historically. They can be studied, as were the Greeks and Romans, only when they come on the historical scene. It is only when they bend the will of the Greco-Roman world that they come on the stage of history. The Romans had been aware of the Jews but had paid no attention to them, or had treated them as curiosities. In the period of Rome's despondency, when it was looking backward for authority and forward through revelation, it was finally willing to listen to the message of the Jews.

Hegel observes that when the people of the west look for happiness beyond this world, in the supernatural, they look past Greece to the east, but when they look for happiness in this world, they look to Greece. The Greeks were the first people in history to seek their happiness in this world. The whole history of the Greco-Roman effort was to attain the highest happiness of man in this world.

It started with Thales and the sophists, progressed through Plato and Aristotle, who defined the instrument of man's salvation as the city-state, and it passed through the collapse of the Greek city state to the Romans, who attempted to salvage the instrument. The sophists were like John Dewey, who believed the real goals of life were to be attained through society. It is society that determines what our life goals ought to be. This applies to all societies, whether democratic, communistic, fascist; all determine what the direction of happiness is.

The Romans learned from the Greeks that the state was necessary for salvation, and worked on the problem of securing it with the best talents available. They found this to be a full-time job. The Romans worked out the end that we usually associate with the goal of the Soviet Union, the only country in the world that contemplates doing away with all its enemies. All the other countries in the west are adherents of the doctrine of multiple sovereignty, using the technique of a balance of powers to survive. If a power on the continent wishes to take England, it must first take the whole continent, for should it fail to do this, all England would need to do to snuff out the threat would be to ally itself with some continental power. It was the German plan to do this. It is the communist plan to eliminate the possibility of war altogether. Not many nations want to do this, because most nations realize that when there is no enemy the power of the nation withers away. The Roman solution, when it was finally achieved, made everybody sad and for the first time in history since it had cut its umbilical cord from the east, the Greco-Roman world began to listen to the east.

The Mediterranean was studded with Greek communities which, as Cicero said, surrounded the Mediterranean like the tassels on a senator's toga. In between the Greek cities were the Semitic communities. The big new element before the turn of the new era were the Jews, who after their dispersion had settled through every major city in the Mediterranean. Their message was heard by cultivated people. The Jews tended to split into two camps: those who were eager to adjust to the Greco-Roman civilization and who spoke Latin and Greek, and the orthodox Jews who did not want to be absorbed in the Greco-Roman world.

During the Diaspora, it became necessary to translate the Jewish bible into Greek, since many Jews had become Hellenized and had lost the ability to speak the Jewish language. The translation of the Old Testament into Greek was to have tremendous influence in the western world.

It was Philo, a Hellenic Jew, skilled in Greek and Roman ways, who was to teach the Christians how to philosophize in the Hellenic manner, a procedure whereby a non-Jew could read Jewish writing in a meaningful way. He learned this method from the Greeks. Not everything the Greeks did was rational. Some things they did were imaginative. But the Greek obsession was to rationalize even their non-rational achievements. Everything the Greek did was touched with reason. Plato said that imaginative literature had no place in the state. But Aristotle pointed out that Plato had too low an estimation of the ability of reason, which could digest fine art as easily as it could digest the heavenly bodies.

Out of the Greek rational critique there emerged the method of allegorical interpretation. It was possible to take the Homeric stories and turn them inside out to make them mean different things. Allegorical interpretation is not the setting up of a new meaning and an artificial correlation between it and a literary work. In Homer and the Tragedies, the Greek would say, thought is present; they are rational works. Every once in a while the veil of fiction would be thin enough to be seen through and reveal the allegorical story underneath, and this story was really another, more profound story. The literal surface had served the function of a sensuous covering to tempt the reader along, and hit him suddenly right between the eyes with the more profound story, and beyond that the still deeper third meaning, the moral of the work, hidden beneath the more profound story. Homer came to be interpreted in this sense as a source book of moral guidance. The Greeks did not work out these strata of meanings completely. They were later to become four levels of meaning: the literal, the allegorical, the moral, and finally, the anagogic, the higher meaning, the divine plan.

When Philo tried to explain the Old Testament to the Greeks, he could say that unlike most other literary works, this work could stand the Greek allegorical test of reason. It was like a great poem that expands as its reader grows, and the more the reader brings to it of his knowledge, the more it means. It has the infinite suggestivity of great poetry which marks the great poem, and like all great poetry, it mirrors all that is brought to it and can take all the interpretation which is brought to bear on it. Philo claimed this book would withstand all the intelligence that the Greeks could put into it.

This approach attracted the Greeks and the Romans of the Diaspora. The homeland Jews did not at first approve of this interpretation, but later came to use this allegorical method of Philo to explain away apparent contradictions in the Bible.

Philo invited the Greeks and Romans to come and look at this book, these fables, which introduce man to God. But the Greek protested that he had already been introduced to God by Anaxagoras, Socrates, Plato and

Aristotle. Philo countered that it would do no harm to look at the view of God recorded in this book. At one point in the history of Philo's people, Moses was told by God to write down the rules they needed for behavior, and these were dictated in such a way that would mean something to a child or a sage or even to a man who hated the rules.

And when Moses asked God who he should say sent him with these rules, the answer, Philo pointed out, was one which the Greeks were better able to understand than some of the Jews. "And Moses said unto God, Behold, when I come unto the children of Israel, and shall say unto them, The God of your fathers hath sent me unto you; and they shall say to me, What is his name? What shall I say unto them? And God said unto Moses, I AM THAT I AM, and he said, Thus shalt thou say unto the children of Israel, I Am hath sent me unto you." (Exodus, 3:13,14)

There has been some scholarly dispute about what the literal translation of the words, "I Am," should be. The import of the words, it is generally agreed, is that which really *is*, or Being. "Being has sent you"; that which really is has sent you — everything else is appearance.

Philo reminded the Greeks how hard it had been for them to reach this conception. Did they remember what difficulty their philosophers had had peeling the layers of the universe, like an onion, until Parmenides finally reached "being"?

Philo asked the Greek what his God was. To this the Greek replied that God is thought. What does he think? The Universe, everything, all that is, this is what God thinks. He is *thought thinking thought*. He is all three things at the same instant, expressed in subject, verb, and object.

Philo pointed out that his God said, "Let there be light," and in that instant there was light. Was this not *thought, thinking thought*, subject, verb and object all at once? The whole doctrine of the trinity is here, to be taken up by Christianity.

The Jews, Philo reminded the Greeks, are interested primarily in behavior, and in the opening pages of Genesis they have set up the problem of human conduct. Here again, Philo could say to the Greeks that they should find it easy to understand his book. Did the Greeks not know that there would be no problem of human conduct if man were born mature? But man is not born mature, and it is pointless to try to explain to him why he should behave in a certain way until he has become able to behave that way, just as it is pointless to discuss the problems of sex with the child who has yet to feel the pangs of adolescence and growth. The time to tell him about it is when he feels it. Before he feels it, it means absolutely nothing to him.

The Greeks knew that everything would have been much easier if God had made man rational to begin with. It is a horrible thing for man to be born with unrestrained appetites. You don't have to teach a kid to get angry. The child is born angry. The whole purpose of his education is to diminish his anger. He passes through four stages. In the first stage he expresses his anger by turning purple from head to foot. In the second stage, when he is about 10 or 11 and has had some education, he throws an occasional tantrum. In the third stage, when he has reached the level of a college junior and things run contrary to his desire, he frowns. In the final stage, when he has reached the culmination of his education and has submitted his doctoral thesis, and the professor who has read it returns it to him with the remark that he has read his paper and found it interesting but is inclined to feel the very opposite of the matter is true, the now fully educated man, without so much as a hint of a frown, quietly replies that he had never looked at it that way. This is what is meant by education. It is the process of restraining the irrational nature with which man was born.

The Greek might protest: Why had not God, who is omnipotent, created man rational to begin with? Philo could reply that the Book explains this. Because in the Book it is written that God had begun the world by creating

Adam and telling him what his job was, and Adam listened to him. God gave Adam a complete course before he turned him loose with his appetites. God warned him that about the only thing he had to worry about was the first appetite he would encounter. This appetite was not too intense; its modern equivalent could be summed up in the phrase, "man's right to knowledge and the free use thereof."

If Adam could have restrained the appetite to know, then God and he could have really gone places, sparing mankind 6000 years of a civilization that has culminated in the H-bomb. But Adam needed a helpmate, and God created one for him, out of his rib. Why out of his rib? Because, the Book says, all men are brothers, and all men are descended, regardless of what scientists may discover, not from several unrelated races, or even from two persons, but from one person. The implication of this straight descent from Adam is simply this: all men are brothers, brothers in innocence and brothers in guilt. And according to Philo, if all men are brothers then there are no more barbarians.

Adam's helpmate, Eve, tried, as women usually do, to help her husband get on in the world. While in the garden, she heard a little voice telling her about that tree the fruit of which God had commanded should not be eaten, the tree of knowledge of good and evil. How much more allegorical could the Bible be than this?

How far should man go in his knowledge of evil? Should the modern psychologist be given the right to the free pursuit of all knowledge? Does he, for instance, have a right to experimentally compare the reactions of different girls as they are being strangled to death, or the sociologist to compare the reactions of girls from the low income group or high income group? Is he not entitled to a grant to pursue this line of research? One never knows to what use theoretical knowledge might be later put. But someone might remind him that this line of research is defined as murder. Well then, what about the historian?

Consider the light he could throw on history if he had free
access to the contents of the strongboxes of our politicians.
But that would be theft. Is it conceivable that there are
some areas of possible knowledge which, even today, the
disinterested scientist should have no access to?

The little voice tempted Eve. It told her that God
had made her in such a way that she was free; this means she
was free to change herself. How could she possibly know
this unless she violated His command? To be free, she had
to exert her freedom by contravening God's command,
instead of blindly obeying. How could she know she would
not be in a better condition then? By violating the command, she would gain knowledge and immortality, the
little voice said.

She had the power to change her nature. She can
see, but all she has to do is gouge her eyes out and she will
be blind. How does she know this would not be preferable?
Just think, the little voice whispered to her, you have the
power to change your nature and gain real immortality
instead of remaining as you are, in custody. So Eve ate the
apple and was changed.

Adam, when he learned what she had done, was
aghast. But they were of the same flesh, they were one,
bone of my bone, flesh of my flesh. When she gave him the
apple to eat, she gave him a choice, to obey God or to
remain loyal to the woman who meant death. And as
Milton described it, Adam concluded that if death con-
sorted with Eve, then death was life; so he ate the apple,
too.

Later, God found Adam and Eve hiding because
they were naked. How could they know they were naked
unless they had eaten from the forbidden tree? Does not
knowledge follow upon the experience of the thing known?
It cannot precede it. Philo again reminded the Greeks that
they had already considered this problem at some length.
Had not Plato in his Phaedrus described human nature as
reason in a runaway chariot drawn by two horses, the

spirited and the appetitive drives?

What the Jews were telling the Greeks was that human nature had not always been reason in a runaway chariot, but that once upon a time, before man had made his fatal decision, he was in charge of the chariot, the way God had made him.

The serpent had told man he could change his nature. God had made man out of nothing. There was a string attached, as to a puppet, from man to God; the string of truth. The serpent had urged him to free himself, to cut the string. He would not become blind or deaf; he would become a free thinker. And in three score and ten he might be able to cut all the strings. This is very hard to do, one has to become a Bertrand Russell, a real free thinker. At first, man had to cut only this one little string. Centuries later, a man was to discover that the mind is not master of its own house. Freud did not have to read very contemporary literature to discover this.

Cutting the string from man to God unleashed all manner of desires in human nature. Lust was the least of these. The ultimate unleashing of desire was the lust to dominate. After man had unleashed himself from the truth, he fell victim to all the inordinate desires.

And this, Philo explained, was the condition in which the Greeks and Romans understood man. In this condition the only thing that could be done was to apply the Greco-Roman remedy, which was to control the appetites from the beginning. If reason is unleashed from the truth, there can be no order in the world. Reason is not equipped for the task of controlling reason. The Greeks and Romans learned that violence checks violence and that by checking violence an opportunity is given for reason to emerge.

Philo reminded the Greeks that in their tragedies they had long been preoccupied with the problem of inherited guilt, which was the central problem of the Old Testament. What is the solution to this problem? The

Greeks had discovered it in their Ethics.

Man, according to the Greeks, is first in a state of restrained behavior. He next achieves a state of occasionally restrained behavior, which is neutral. Then he progresses to a condition of being habitually restrained. That is to say, he is trained to do the right thing so well that it requires no effort, but is an automatic habit, and this the Greeks called virtue. In this condition, the intellect is released to pursue the truth, which Philo reminded them was the insight that God runs the world, insight into necessity. Virtue is not virtue if it is painful.

There are three phases of moral development. In the first phase, man walks a tightrope and keeps falling off. In the second, he makes an effort, through practice, not to fall off so often. In the third, his habit of walking the tightrope is so well established that he does not have to give it any thought. This is virtue or excellence or, as the Greeks called it, *ârete*. Does not moral excellence become progressively easier? Is an achievement to be thought superior if it is made to look difficult? Quite the contrary. Training means that by repeated effort, a man becomes able not only to make a difficult feat look easy, but actually to be easy. Is not the best football player, or basketball player, or concert pianist the one who is most graceful, who makes his achievement appear spontaneous? This criterion of ease of execution applies to moral excellence also.

The object of moral excellence is that it should not appear difficult. Neither is it an end in itself. Its purpose is to become so automatic as to release the intellect from preoccupation with it.

This is what both the Greeks and the Jews meant, to be habitually virtuous. To be courageous is to do what reason dictates at the right time, and to do it habitually. All virtue, to the Greeks, consists in avoiding extremes. One extreme of courage is cowardliness, the other is foolhardiness; the mean between the two, which reason must locate and virtue must achieve habitually, is courage.

It is not courageous to face 250 tanks with a bow and arrow. Courage means to do the right act for the right reason at the right time. It is an act, as all virtue is, of restraint. The principle behind Jewish ethics is obedience to the rules of behavior. The reason for obedience cannot be demanded before the habit of obedience is achieved. God says you have cataracts on your eyes. Do not ask to see before you have removed the cataracts. The first step is to learn to do the right thing, and afterward you will learn why you have done it. The doctrine of both the Greeks and the ancient Jews is that virtue consists of doing the right thing before the reason for doing it is known.

Adam was in the reverse position. He knew from the start why he was to do the right thing and the appetites came second. But after his fall, the appetites came first and reason second. When Adam cast his lot with Eve, he was giving expression to the antithesis of what God had told him to do. God had not commanded him to love his fellow man, but to love his God above all else.

God had created Adam, Eve, and the serpent, and they were all puppets. How then, is it possible to blame man, who was created by God, for his own fall?

God had created man free, attached to Himself, as a puppet, by the thread of truth. But man cut the thread and ran amuck. Man wanted to know he was really free. The only way that he could be certain was to violate God's command. God said, do not eat of the fruit of that tree. And yet, how could man really know that he had the freedom of reaching out and plucking the fruit? What if there was some in-built counter-mechanism in his nature, that would check his arm from plucking the fruit? He had to dare God and reach out for the fruit and see if he could eat it. How else to know freedom, except by exerting it? After man had established his freedom by cutting the thread of truth, the only course left for him was to try to reestablish that original condition which did not appear to be freedom, in which he appeared to be in custody, but which really was the ultimate freedom, the freedom that comes from insight into necessity.

Parents usually put stern prohibitions on the child. The child is confined within many rules that restrict its behavior. If the child wants to exert its sense of freedom, it violates these prohibitions, only to find that in their violation are latent many unforeseen complications. The child may in time even come to suspect that to have done willingly what its parents had commanded is real freedom.

What is the answer to this problem? Consider the dilemma of Abraham, to whom God spoke, commanding that he kill his son. Abraham did what Adam could not do. He obeyed. The first law is to love God with your whole heart. But what is the good? The good is that which God commands.

The Greeks asked, what does one get from such blind obedience? Philo replied that the result of such obedience was an insight not very different from what Plato had called the Vision of the Good.

The history of the world since the Judaification of Rome has been an effort to undo its Judaification. How did the secularist world of antiquity succumb?

We examined the message of the Jews of the Diaspora. These were Jews who were thoroughly Hellenized and their doctrine was tinged in every part with Hellenism, saturated with Greek culture.

The Jews had two messages. There was the same dichotomy among the Jews then as now. There were the Jews of the Diaspora, who required a standard to live up to while they were assimilating another culture, and there were the Jews of the Homeland. The Diaspora Jew's message was universalistic, while that of the homeland Jew's was nationalistic and particularistic. These two aspects of Judaism are incompatible, yet Judaism has had to suffer them.

For 150 years before the Maccabees, Judaism had

been universalistic. After the Maccabees came the particularistic homeland Jew. The message of the Homeland Jew was precise: he was trying to live up to the 613 laws. The reward for obeying God was not vague for the particularistic Jew. The message of the Jew of the Diaspora was philosophical and reminiscent of Plato and Aristotle. It was the rewards of the homeland Jew which made the Romans sit up and take notice. His goal is expressed in Micah:

> But in the last days it shall come to pass, that the mountain of the house of the Lord shall be established in the top of the mountains, and it shall be exalted above the hills; and people shall flow unto it. And many nations shall come, and say, Come, and let us go up to the mountain of the Lord, and to the house of the God of Jacob; and he will teach us of his ways, and we will walk in his paths: for the law shall go forth of Zion, and the word of the Lord from Jerusalem.
>
> And he shall judge among many people, and rebuke strong nations afar off; and they shall beat their swords into plowshares, and their spears into pruning-hooks; nation shall not lift up a sword against nation, neither shall they learn war any more. (4: 1, 2, 3)
>
> Now also many nations are gathered against thee, that say, Let her be defiled and let our eye look upon Zion. But they know not the thoughts of the Lord, neither understand they his counsel; for he shall gather them as sheaves into the floor. Arise and thresh, O daughter of Zion, for I will make thine horn iron, and I will make thine hoofs brass; and thou shalt beat in pieces many people; and I will consecrate their gain unto the Lord, and their substance unto the Lord of the whole earth. (4: 11, 12, 13)

If this passage is interpreted literally, it represents the aspiration of that small community to give law to the world, just as the Romans had done.

A favorite psalm of St. Augustine, the 137th psalm of David, says:

> By the rivers of Babylon, there we sat down, yea, we wept,

when we remembered Zion. We hanged our harps upon the willows in the midst thereof. For there they that carried us away captive required of us a song; and they that wasted us required of us mirth, saying Sing us one of the songs of Zion. How shall we sing the Lord's song in a strange land? If I forget thee, O Jerusalem, let my right hand forget her cunning. If I do not remember thee, let my tongue cleave to the roof of my mouth; if I prefer not Jerusalem above my chief joy. Remember, O Lord, the children of Edom in the day of Jerusalem, who said, raze it, raze it, even to the foundation thereof.

O daughter of Babylon, who art to be destroyed, happy shall he be that rewardeth thee as thou hast served us. Happy shall he be, that taketh and dasheth thy little ones against the stones.

If this passage is not interpreted allegorically, it makes one wince.

The Romans were roused to tremendous anxiety and activity by anyone among the Jews claiming to be the Messiah. The Maccabean revolution was fresh in their minds. After the Romans had vanquished the Maccabeans, any uprising of the Jews was dealt heavy blows.

It was on this basis that the Jewish message of the Diaspora created such a disturbance. For what was the national aspiration of the Jews? It was nothing else but the conversion of the world to their law, a dream of a world monarchy. The Romans rose up whenever a claimant appeared. It was only Judea — not any other nation — that was incompatible with Roman sovereignty.

The Greco-Roman response, which is to say the response of the Roman with a Greek mentality, as well as of the Greek, to the pleasant message of the Jews of the Diaspora was to note the similarity of the Jewish God to the Zeus of past omnipotence. Why, the Greek questioned, should the Jew be so different as to have been singled out by God and given commandments to obey which would enable him to achieve this new faculty, a vision of God? The secret of the Jews was salvation not through the state or political entity, but by obedience to the commandments of God,

The Greek remembered well what he had done with his own gods. Prometheus had spoken for the Greek spirit against Zeus, who had played with the Greeks as with toys. He protested the unfairness of Zeus and swore that nothing could undo his protest. The victory of Prometheus over the omnipotence of Zeus was his withholding of love from Zeus. This symbolized the general rejection of God by the Greek mentality. For he who had created all had also created all the sins of man and bore the ignominious guilt for his creation. He was the vilest of things, notwithstanding all his power. This protest is found in Prometheus and in the epicureans.

It was not possible for the Jew to allegorize too long with the Greek. The Jew had a ready reply for the Greek. If God was responsible for all, if he was the author of all men's suffering, if the curse the Greek hurled at him was valid, then he was the author of that curse as well and it was thereby reduced to nothing. The very God that the Greek was cursing had pulled the curse from his tongue.

The other alternative of the Greco-Roman response was to deny that God exists. Man knows but one thing: the world is indifferent to him. It grinds him to an eternal death and life holds nothing good. Every struggle brings defeat. No one can penetrate the vast veil, for behind it there is no light. All is vanity, nothingness. This was the characteristic mood of the ancient world, described by the historian Windelband as the "agony of the Ancient world."

The Greeks had removed divinity from behavior and explanation and put it into art. They took matters into their own hands, and made the state the highest glory.[32]

The Roman response to the message of the homeland Jew was more simple. The Roman accused the Jew of being a dreamer. Was it not the Roman who had made everybody peace loving? Had he not already done that of which Israel was only dreaming? The Roman could say to Israel that it was he, not the Jew, who had what the Jew who depended on supernatural power was looking for. We, the masters of the world, he might add, have the king-size headache. The Roman could see, in the words of Micah, his own prophesy. Micah had said, "Many nations are gathered against thee," and he had prophesied, "Thou shall beat in pieces many people." Had not the Roman fulfilled all this? Had not the world submitted to him? There are two ways a people can submit. They can submit willingly, or they can go under the "hoofs of brass."

A wise people knows that peace must be enforced with force. The Roman jurists calculated just how much force was needed to enforce peace. The amount of force which was needed was more than anybody else had.

Whenever there was any hint of a Jewish Messiah, Rome sent out its legions to see how he would withstand them. The Romans wanted to enforce a stoic peace, but the ancient Jews felt the same way about a stoic peace as Ben Gurion would feel about it. Peace simply means that there will be no fighting. And this is what the Roman peace had accomplished. The Romans objected to the messianic aspiration of the Jews.

When a nation has defined a nucleus of sovereignty, it passes through three phases. First, it drives the invader from its land, next it sets up limits about its boundaries which are inviolable, and finally in the third phase it pushes out, in order to make the world a safe place in which it can exist. In Isaiah and in Micah, there is a clear contemplation of this third phase.

Either the Romans had completely misunderstood the Jews or they had a particular malevolence for them. Only in Judea, and not elsewhere, was there a claim to political right. There was a feeling of a coming messianic kingdom. To the Romans the Jews seemed to be agitators who, without visible means, were able to will to fight, without manpower, because they believed the hand of God would guide them. It was with this Jewish nationalistic aspiration in the background that the Greco-Roman rejected the first wave of the Judaic invasion.

Following the first Judaic invasion, the Jews made a second attack on Rome through a more subtle fellow. He disclaimed the Jewish nationalist message. He came from Tarsus. He spoke for the Jews, but not as one who threatens. He asked the Greeks and Romans not to mix identity. He did not speak for the Jews who wanted to rule. He brought, he said, the answer that the Greco-Roman world needed in terms it could understand. He did not bring the Judaic help which came crushingly from above, but a help which came through eternity, had come into time, through man.

The Jews require a sign; the Greeks seek after wisdom. But Paul preached neither signs nor wisdom. Paul preached "Christ crucified." Had not Socrates sought after wisdom and tried out of intellectual intercourse to reach a higher truth? The man from Tarsus said that he had that kind of truth.

Paul addressed the Greeks and Romans with his message. He was a storyteller and the story was written down. He told a story about a just man whose betrothed was unaccountably with child, how a voice dissuaded this man from putting her away privily and told him to take Mary, who had conceived a child by the holy spirit, as his wife. The child was not an ordinary child. He was involved, as Paul said, in his father's business, astonished learned rabbis with his conversation, became a carpenter, and always spoke about how things had to change.

Aristotle had long before summed up what a man needed and wanted in this world. He had said that all men by nature desire to be happy, desire to know, and desire the life of the political community. When this man was asked what he was going to do for the world, he answered: "I am the way (happiness), I am the truth (knowledge), I am the life (political community). Those who listened to this man and followed him, believing he was the way to happiness, found that his way led to being arrested, tried, convicted and sentenced. His way led to the cross. When he was hung on the cross, his followers pleaded for a sign. But there was no sign. He spoke to a thief at his side, promising him that that day he would be at his side in paradise. He pleaded for his persecutors, asking that they be forgiven because they knew not what they did. He cried out to God, "Why hast thou forsaken me?" and he bled and died.

He had said that the kingdom was here, and they buried him. Later a white-clad figure at his tomb announced that he was gone. His followers came to make inquiries, and a story began to circulate that it would be their task to take the religion of Abraham, Isaac and Jacob, which this man had simplified from 613 laws to two laws, and spread it to the far corners of the world.

It would be unreasonable to question the historical existence of Jesus or his general character as depicted in the gospels. For most historians, any conclusions concerning this are irrelevant. The primary historical reality from the Greco-Roman standpoint was that it was Paul of Tarsus who spoke of Jesus for the first time, to the Romans. He couldn't claim to be an eye witness to Jesus, nor could he have conceived of his kingdom coming into this world so quietly by reading the Bible. Happiness is dying with Jesus and suffering with Jesus.

After Jesus had returned to life, he invited his followers to join him in body by eating him. Many abandoned him because this appeared too distasteful. Peter, who had no place to go, stayed.

Paul said of Jesus that one did not choose him, but that it was he who chose those who would follow him. "None can get to my father except through me, but none can get to me lest my father drag him."

Paul had in fact been trying to stamp out the Christian foolishness, this preaching that the Messiah had arrived and that the kingdom of God was established, when he was suddenly knocked off his horse and blinded by a dazzling light. This was how Jesus chose his followers. (From now on you work for me!) The God of Abraham, Isaac and Jacob, who had made men out of nothing, had done another arbitrary thing and assumed human form. Who could believe it? Not many Jews believed it.

Some people would later say, as did Nietzche, that Christianity was invented by the Jews to teach the Gentiles to turn the other cheek. But if one argues against the historical authenticity of Christianity, which is to say the actual existence of Christ, it nonetheless remains obvious that at some moment Christianity came to be, since it is still here with as.

When St. Paul was asked why the Jews did not believe in Christ, he explained that if all Jews believed in Christ, then no one else would believe in him. But after the whole world had heard of Christ, then the Jews who had opened the doors for him would also join him and these would be the last days.

When one later finds Constantine accepting Christianity, one must wonder what really happened. What a miracle all this would have been if no historical Christ had existed!

For a time there were Jewish Christians and non-Jewish Christians. After Paul the Christians were called the third people, neither Jews nor Gentiles, but a liberal intermediate people. These intermediate people called upon the Greco-Romans to accept the God whom they rejected, and urged the Jews to reject their extreme nationalism.

It is not difficult to see how the stoic mentality could be attracted to Christianity, which came as a combination of these two peoples.

We have looked at Christianity from the Greek and Roman view. We have examined the impression it made on Greco-Romans. That is why we began with St. Paul. Anything that was supposed to have been said before him was framed by the church authorities after him. The best historians agree that the message of St. Paul contains the entire germ of Christianity.

Christianity appealed among the Jews to the most lowly people, not to the upper classes. It was a leveling doctrine. The major political objection usually made against the Jew, which is hard to state and is so often obscured, is that he is a leveler.

A leveler is one who calls attention to the anatomy of a society, pointing out that there is a head on top and that there are feet on the bottom. The feet on the bottom represent the underdog. When the Jew enters a community, he tends to level society.

There are different varieties of Judaism, the orthodox, the conservative, the reformed, but the most leveling of all Jewish sects is Christianity. The Christian who recognizes no master or slave tends to destroy the whole hierarchy of the state.

The Jew is a leveler. If a religious element is alienated from political office, what effect will this have in society? There will be a tendency on the part of the religious element to sympathize with the liberal leveling process. Leveling does not mean the motives of the leveler are bad. It simply means that he is there and social duress will not remove him. One can turn up the fires but the leveling element will not melt, just as the Arabs in present day Israel will not melt. Leveling makes it impossible for a state to form a hierarchy that will survive.

Among the Jews, the Pharisees despised the lower classes and caused the lower classes to fall into ignorance. This helped to strengthen Christianity among the lower classes. Jesus spoke to the Jews as a Jew, but the Jewish nationalists looked on him with suspicion. The Christian movement called for the abandonment of the earthly kingdom. It did not need a political kingdom on earth. It was a doctrine dangerous to the homeland Jew and made Christianity unacceptable to him.

Homeland Judaism calls for political formation, at least in the homeland. The Torah is not concerned with matters of faith alone; it combines a concern for religion with a concern for law, justice, science and matter, and the state as well. Herein consists the weakness of Judaism and the reason why the Jews did not develop the secular arts or jurisprudence. But here too is the strength of Judaism, for it broke down the wall between religion and daily life. What was holy was brought down to earth.

When the Jews rose up with their Messiah, the Romans had great hostility for them. There was fierce fighting against enormous odds. After the destruction of the Jewish state, when it could no longer be considered as a nationalistic threat to their sovereignty, the Romans extended tolerance even to the Jews, who were the only intolerant people in the empire. The Romans would have even put the Jewish images in the Pantheon. All they asked was that the Jew pour the libation and take the oath to the divinity of the emperor. They did not even ask the Jew to believe the oath.

After the state of Judah had been destroyed, the Romans were willing to make an agreement with the Jews. The Jews were levelers everywhere except in their own homeland, where they aspired to a kingdom of their own. The Christians refused to accept the Jewish distinction. The Christian kingdom, unlike the Jewish, was not of this world, and was consequently even more leveling.

The Roman sensed the difference in the response of the Jews to the legal relationships of Rome, and he defined his legal relation to the Jew. He gave to the Jew the rights of a Roman citizen, but since the Jew refused the right of worshipping the genius of Rome and since he persisted in his desire for a nation of his own, he would be a citizen who would be discriminated against. This Roman arrangement, legally defined, was between the Roman and a man who had a mixed allegiance. The Roman definition of the Jew, deriving from his refusal to swear the oath, was a dual relationship. It made of the Jew both an alien and a citizen at the same time.

Into this picture came the Jew who was also a Christian. He too refused to swear the oath. When the Roman asked the Jewish Christian if his refusal to take the oath was because he, like the Jews, was loyal to the Jewish nation, his reply was "No, his kingdom was not of this world." To this the Roman said that the Christian was not entitled to the immunity of the Jew. To make matters worse, in so many cases the Christian was not a Jew at all, but a native-born Roman who wouldn't swear the oath. They wanted the rights of the Jews with the immunity of the Jews, but these were not Jews of the flesh; these were Romans. With this realization, a fury came over the Romans.

There are meager references to the contacts between the Romans and the early Christians. Tacitus refers to them in his account of Nero. But there is not much more than this. By the time of the exchange of letters between Trajan and Pliny, the Christians must have been around a long time to provoke such correspondence. The question is raised by Pliny whether a Christian should be punished for not having done anything, but for just being a Christian. In this exchange of letters (about 110 A.D.), the Emperor Trajan does not say not to kill the Christians but rather to give them the benefit of the doubt if they care to deny that they are Christians.

The first contact between the Roman police and the Christians was to protect the Christians against the hatred of their own neighbors. At first the Roman soldiers defended them. The Christian Sunday repasts on the flesh and blood of Christ aroused a popular indignation against them, but for a long time there were no persecutions.

With Tertullian's conversion to Christianity, we get that explanation of Christianity which convinced the Roman world. Tertullian, a Roman lawyer, looked at the world with naked eyes and learned it is a sad world. Most people who observe would agree that the world is full of sound and fury signifying nothing. How can one justify this life? The Jew says it is justifiable, that someday we will all live in a land of milk and honey. But after everyone is taken care of by Medicare, will this justify all the past illnesses that have been neglected? What about all the Jews that had never reached the land of milk and honey? Who, in brief, can justify this play told by an idiot? Suppose that God, who had written the play, wanted to justify it. The story of what he would have to do would be the story of Christianity; Christianity tries to justify this tale.

Oliver Goldsmith knew how to help poverty. He would visit the destitute people and become so appalled at their condition that he would faint. In the end, the destitute would have to revive and take care of Oliver Goldsmith. The best way to help poverty is to make it help you.

Let us not deceive ourselves into thinking that all the backward, underprivileged nations that are now receiving our CARE packages are not quietly waiting for the day when we will be down and out and they can send CARE packages to us.

This is what God did. He went down among the people who thought they were badly off and assumed the worst role among them. He took the role of a Jew, not a normal Jew who was merely despised by all peoples, but a Jew that the Jews themselves were ashamed to call a Jew. How much lower could he be than that? He let humanity give him the worst treatment. He gave humanity a strange satisfaction. He took the blame for everything by admitting that he was guilty for this whole meaningless play, and humanity pinned him to a cross. Humanity could never, after this, complain of how badly off it was, for the creator himself had put himself into the worst role of all, and assumed the guilt and punishment for the suffering of humanity. But was not God just playing a role? After all, he is God and not man. Was this not merely a part God was playing? A part that he could step out of?

Let us remember that while he was pinned to the cross Christ cried out, "My God, my God, why has thou forsaken me?" God had shut himself off forever from the love of God and though his followers might not believe it, and though they would join his body, they would feel from time to time very strange. Were the followers of Christ, as Luther was to question, really so certain that they were saved? If they were, then they had not really been with Christ.

If it had not been for this explanation of Christ, Christianity would have been quickly swept into the Mediterranean. This was the doctrine that won the Greco-Roman world. It was the tremendous appeal of this negative moment of Christianity, when Christ himself was denied the love of God, that took the secularist par excellence. It was from this that Christianity derived its power in the Greco-Roman world. The Christian message seemed to say that either man had turned his back on God or God had turned his back on man. Tertullian summed up his position by saying that he knew his explanation was absurd, but that if it were not absurd, if it were rational, he would not have been able to believe it, to have faith in the substance of things hoped for, in the evidence of things unseen.

The Romans after Caesar and Augustus were primarily interested in getting the consent of the people. The first basis of consent, that of Augustus, derived from the sheer horror the Roman experienced when he considered the civil wars, and proscriptions which would result without an Augustus.

But was there no better basis for consent?

The Romans tried to resurrect the good old religions. They began philosophizing, giving rise to the movement of Neo-platonism. They tried to treat the religions, the popular legends of Rome, the way Philo had treated the Old Testament and the Greeks had read Homer; they tried to rationalize them. The Roman was trying to build up a positive spirit for a people living in peace to live by.

The third century A.D. was a century of political chaos and Rome was making an effort to rally the populace around some banner. It is with this background that the Roman intellectual controversy with Christianity occurs.

Between St. Paul and Constantine, two great intellectual polemics against Greco-Roman Christianity took place. The first was that of Celsus, a distinguished popular writer who chided his fellow Greeks and Romans for having been taken in by Christianity. The second was that of Porphyry.

Celsus did not object to the Jews; they had a quality that the Roman could admire. They were, at least, patriotic to their own nation. But this is exactly what the Christians did not have, patriotism to a nation,

The arguments of Celsus against the Christians who were not Jews were to become the foundation for the much later attacks of Voltaire upon Christianity. Celsus argues that the Christians forever talk about the kingdom of God, but whom do they invite into it? Usually men who band together to implement a solemn enterprise seek out the best among themselves to assure the success of that enterprise. Whom do Christians invite? They invite the sinners, the foolish, the simple-minded, the unfortunate and the unjust. If one wanted to put together an assemblage of robbers and the lowest dregs of society, he would find them banded together as Christians.

And where, Celsus asks, is this vaunted kingdom of theirs? They say it is not of this world. Do they live in it? No, they do not live within their own kingdom, nor do they live in the Roman kingdom, but they wander between two worlds, the Roman world and the heavenly world. Reason demands that they choose one or the other. If they persist in refusing to take the oath to Rome, they should be willing to be cut down and dispatched with utmost haste to their own kingdom. If, on the other hand, they wish to enjoy the life of this world, to marry and raise children, they should be willing to pay honor to those who have these temporal things in their care; they should be willing to support the Roman emperor, to maintain the empire.

Tertullian, who was a contemporary of Celsus, tried to answer him on behalf of the Christians. The main answer, however, came from the Greek philosopher Origen, who wrote a book entitled *Against Celsus*. Origen wrote about 60 years after Tertullian. The value of Origen's work was that it was to become the main source of our knowledge of Celsus, the writings of Celsus having been lost.

Origen replies to Celsus that he is correct. It is true that only sinners are allowed among the Christians. But this is because the sinner is sick and Christianity is a hospital to cure the sick.

The reason, Origen continues, that the Christian does not take the advice of Celsus and does not dispatch himself to his other kingdom is that his law prohibits it. He must not commit suicide. But, Origen reminds Celsus, the Christian does not depend, as Celsus seems to think, on Rome for his material existence. He is quite capable, in his own community, of taking care of himself materially. He has even constructed a complete hierarchy that parallels the Roman hierarchy. For every official occupying a post in the Roman empire, the Christian has a similar official occupying a similar post in the church. To this the Pagan could only respond with apprehension. It would seem that the Christian really wanted to take over his world after all.

The Christian, Origen says, intends to continue living in the community. He would continue to educate his sons and participate in his community. He did not intend to pay tribute, however, to the idols of this world. He would rather pray to become an imitator of Christ.

Origen observed that the Christian knew that in each city there was a different nation, a nation of God. The Christian had his own hierarchy of officials to serve that other nation. But the difference between the Christian hierarchy and the Roman hierarchy was that the Christians thrust the authority of office on men whose object was humility, whereas the Roman hierarchy was comprised of men who were ambitious for power. The Christian was not ambitious for power nor did he seek office. This was the prototype for all the later day politicians who claim they did not choose to run for office—and have to be ordered to run.

It was the presence of the Christian hierarchy that led the Roman authority to interpret Christianity as a much greater threat than Judaism. The Jews had an identity. They had a nation, a physical state, or aspired toward a nation in this world. But the Christians had constructed a phantom government renouncing the use of force, representing a kingdom not of this world. It was a sovereignty that paralleled the Roman sovereignty and appeared fully able to take over all activities sufficient for human life, if the Roman civic government should collapse.

Under Decius, in 249 A.D. there was a tremendous persecution of the Christians. The Romans clearly realized that Christianity had an imperial unity and that their communication was good enough to have an effect. It was clear that this organization could be a terrible menace to Rome. Tertullian had protested that the Christian institution was not a state like other states which were built on force. It was not a threat; it only wanted to abandon emperor worship.

Decius had been indiscriminate in his persecution. The Emperor Valerian tried to conduct persecution on a more statesmanlike level. The flock itself was exempt from death; only the leaders and Roman converts were condemned to die. This approach was destined to wear out.

The basis for the great administrative struggle between the Roman empire and the church was developing. On the one hand, there were the imperial offices under the Emperor. On the other hand, Christianity moved in and developed counterparts to the imperial offices. Were the emperor one day to be converted to Christianity, the office of the papacy would be latent in the situation. Administratively, the church fitted itself into the Roman system, awaiting its collapse. It would one day inherit the Roman administrative system—when the Roman political system would come to exist only in law books.

Unlike the Roman conversion to Christianity, which began at the bottom with prostitutes, slaves and the destitute who gradually reached the highest classes, the opposite was to happen with the Germanic tribes, who were not converted from the bottom, but from the top, from Clovis down.

Porphyry was the last great Neo-Platonist. He tried to keep alive the popular image of Plato and systematize in terms of the Aristotelian concept of nature. He intended to philosophize the religious sentiment of antiquity and thereby preserve it; Plato especially lends himself to this kind of an undertaking.

Porphyry wrote powerful things which had an influence in the Middle Ages. Among the things he wrote was a great polemic against Christianity. He defined what was acceptable from Christianity and what was not acceptable to the Roman intellect. Many things were acceptable but a few were not. Porphyry as an opponent of Christianity remains unanswered. His main arguments against Christianity have to do with three basic Christian beliefs.

The opening sentences of St. John have a Philonic ring: "In the beginning there was the Word." The Neo-Platonist recognized the term "word" as "logos", but the objection of Porphyry was that the Logos should have come down and taken on flesh. This was a contention that was hard to defend philosophically. It was hard to be rationally impressed by it.

The second objection of Porphyry was against the Christian doctrine of creation, the contention that God had created the world of matter out of nothing, as the Old Testament says. This was hard to accept rationally. This concept, however, is not so repugnant to reason if it is viewed from the Aristotelian and Hegelian viewpoints, that the nothing out of which the something is made is potentially something. The child is not the man, in that sense he is not something, or is nothing, but that he is a potential nothing or a potential something. The doctrine of potentiality, however, has been resisted by the disciples of pure nothingness, more than infidelity.

The third objection of Porphyry was against the Christian belief in the resurrection of the Flesh. Porphyry could not believe that the Christians were being honest. This was the most offensive belief.

Plato had developed in his *Phaedo* the pessimistic view that this life was a prison-house. The whole problem of Platonic ethics consisted in enabling man to pull himself out of the flesh so that he might be face to face with the eternal forms. This attracted the Neo-Platonist as a logical goal for man. After a man had succeeded in doing this, what greater reward could there be? What could the resurrection of the flesh possibly add to a soul confronting the eternal forms? The concept of resurrected flesh Porphyry viewed as a doctrine intended to appeal to the masses.

Early Christianity was distinguished from Philonic Judaism and Neo-Platonism primarily by one principle and nothing else, and this one principle was the "incarnation of the logos." It was this principle, the incarnation of the Lord, Christ as Christ in the Lord, that the Greco-Roman intellectual had such a difficult time accepting. It was not a contribution made by the pagans.

In its efforts to answer the polemic of Porphyry, the church did the same thing as he did. The church accepted what was acceptable to the Christian in pagan thinking and merely isolated the points of difference.

The combatant who would win this argument would not go back to the original little doctrine, but would take the entire bag and baggage of the enemy. It was in this fight that Greco-Roman Christianity was shaped. The work of

Porphyry was pushed aside by the church, but not until it had been answered. The major critic of Porphyry was to be St. Augustine.

St. Augustine was to thank Porphyry for introducing him to a knowledge of God. He learned about God from the Neo-Platonists. The only thing he could not learn from the pagan was the scandal of the incarnation.

Behind this intellectual struggle was the illegal hierarchy of the church. The ecclesiastic formation was accomplished illegally; the state did not advance it. While on one level the church formed its philosophical doctrine, on another it formed its structural order.

After the death of Porphyry, the Roman Empire made a last effort to smash Christianity and reorganize the state. This was the work of Diocletian. Diocletian was a tremendous figure in the history of the world. He succeeded in pulling the state together.

Diocletian introduced into the state a new technique, a compulsion to the performance of duties. He began talking as one who sees the necessity of regulating industry and labor. The problem in the Roman state was to get people to work. This is the problem which Diocletian approached

There was a tremendous movement of money. Diocletian extracted relief aids from the money. When money gets into the hands of the lowest level, business and industry flourish off their marginal pleasures. Diocletian took a real hand in legislation, at the same time defending the cause. On moralistic grounds and with high purpose, he introduced price controls. He also began to introduce something which had been latent since the Pax, a kind of Oriental serfdom or caste system which would determine who would work at what job from a centralized point of view.

A man was compelled to ply the trade of his father. The men were kept on the farms and in the unions whether they liked it or not. They were not unwilling, however, because everybody else was being constrained.

Diocletian recognized the need for some principle that would justify this centralized interpretation of economic life by an identification with the good of the nation as a whole. He tried to generate a religious atmosphere to combat the depression of minds that is augmented wherever a caste system is inaugurated. He tried to bolster Neo-Platonism which had adapted so much from Judaism, even its singing and chanting, that it appeared almost identical with it in its external form. But it became progressively clear that although large sums of money were being poured into Neo-Platonism to make it a positive ground for the economic measures of the state, it simply was not going to work.

With respect to the illegal religions in the Empire, the Emperor had the power to crucify them, and also the power to release them. Up until now the Romans had used only one of their powers, the power to crucify.

With Constantine, Rome decided to try the other approach, that of releasing the Christians. Constantine emerges as a benefactor of Christianity. It is impossible to consider Constantine without asking why he had inaugurated this new approach.

Constantine found that the Christian church was not prostrate from its persecutions; he did not have to raise the church from the dust. The church was vigorous; all the resistance of the state had been to no avail. The church flourished and all the attacks upon it by the state were not supported by public opinion. The customary policy of persecution which Rome had followed was replaced by Constantine's decree of toleration (311). Constantine did not make Christianity an official religion of the state. He just released Christianity to do as it wanted, to worship as it pleased. Many Christians, such as Justin the Martyr, had asked for tolerance. They had argued that while people in the empire were free to worship all kinds of absurd objects, the Christians were condemned to death because they used the name of Christ, even though all that they said was essentially the same as had been said by the Greeks before them.

Constantine's decree of toleration accorded to all Christians as well as to all other faiths, full liberty to pursue the religion of their consciences, whatever it might be. This was typical of the Roman indifference to religion. They did not care what a man worshipped as long as he was a good citizen.

They made a compromise with the Christians as they had earlier made with the Jews. With this toleration decree the illegality of Christianity was to come to an end. This was to be a turning point with tremendous repercussions.

The Christian was respectable now, and the old-time Christians looked down at the softies that were coming into the church now that it was a legal institution. These new people were doing positive, agreeable things. These were the kind of men whom one might expect to write books on the satisfaction of being a Christian.

The aversion of the old-timers to the softies created an intense puritanical reaction in the church, culminating in an effort to get rid of the people who had drifted into the church for personal gain. The old-timers preferred the days when the church was persecuted. Persecutions got rid of corrupt people in the church. Only diehards stick through thick and thin. At least, under duress, the church had diehards in it whose motives were pure. This intense puritanical movement is reminiscent of the critical controversy between Peter and Paul. Peter had wanted to make Christianity a tougher religion to get into; Paul wanted everyone in the world to join.

In an effort to remain in a persecuted status, this movement culminated in North Africa with a group called the Donatists. This group represented one of the most significant movements in western history. It involved the famous incident of a Christian bishop surrendering the names of his parishioners, an incident which was amplified after Christianity had been legalized. The question of whether people who had been ordained by a morally corrupt bishop were really ordained, and whether these ordained could administer baptism, began to circulate among the Christians. The answer of the puritans was that they were not really ordained, and that they must be re-ordained before they could administer baptism.

It took a long time for the church to resolve this issue. Eventually the church was to hold that the moral quality of a man who administered the sacraments did not bear on the efficacy of the sacraments; a drunken priest is as good as a saint for administering the sacraments.

Render unto God the things that are God's and unto Caesar the things that are Caesar's. But what if Caesar should become a Christian?

The first emperor who was truly Christian was Constantius. He gave the church a real headache because he raised the inevitable question: "Is the church in the empire or is the empire in the church"? This remained a crucial question until our own time when it was finally settled. There is no state in the world today where the church is held above the state. The Vatican does not have political power.

The first episode surrounding the name of Constantius, a born Christian, was that he had at one time ordered a minority of bishops who were bickering at a council convened in the east, to submit or be exiled. He appointed new bishops to attain unanimity. In the west a similar dispute arose when a Roman bishop reminded the emperor not to confound his absolute will with the canons of the church. When, asked the bishop, had the emperor decided matters of the church? When had a priest ever consulted the emperor? When had the church owed obedience to the Emperor?

It was at this time that the primacy of the Roman

bishop was established. For the most part, the authority of the Roman church was favored by the Christian community. But the churches of the empire had till then been like sisters. Rome was now to become the mother.

The Roman church pulled its rank. By the time the illegal period of Christianity was over, the bishop of Rome was accepted as the head of the Christian community, the direct disciple of Peter.

Milan was the site of another great crisis. An interesting man emerged from there, the first man of genuine political ability to be in the church.

The orthodox Christians made a bid for the Cathedral of Milan, creating great civil disturbances. This up-and-coming man, with a bright political future, was chosen by the civil authorities to investigate the dispute. Ambrose, a scholar from a Christian family, had not been baptized. He was young. He made such a fine figure and addressed the people in the squares with such mastery that he quickly became their favorite. The Emperor ordered this man, later to be known as St. Ambrose, to respond to the people's political appeals, and made him a bishop. This was the last time that this happened. The situation is not unlike the position of Thomas Beckett, the Archbishop of Canterbury, later examined by T. S. Eliot in *Murder in the Cathedral*.

The emperor had created a bishop, and he expected him to command the universal respect of all parties. Ambrose was in a similar situation. The people hailed Ambrose and wanted him made an archbishop.

In his writings the church became rhetorical, and he raised the relationship of the church to the state to a political level. It was as a consequence of the later conflict between Ambrose and the Emperor that the church began to realize its political power while the emperor lost his.

The big crisis came with the eastern emperor, the elder Theodosius, who wanted to run both church and state.

The church claimed the right to interpret Jesus. It never denied that the state had the right to crucify Christianity. The church affirmed that the state had the legal right to abolish Christianity; and if it had the right to abolish Christianity, it also had the right to abolish the other religions.

The incident involving Theodosius stemmed from his taking 500 hostages in the Balkans and killing them to compensate for ten Romans who had been killed, and then taking 500 more hostages. Theodosius indulged himself in an excessive slaughtering of hostages. Ambrose exercised his authority and excommunicated him from the church.

He did not question the Emperor's right to kill or not to kill hostages, but he condemned him for rejoicing in the slaughter. Ambrose invited Theodosius to kill him, too. The great popularity of Ambrose deterred Theodosius; he dared not kill Ambrose, but he laid siege to his cathedral. It became apparent, however, that this move would not be successful. The Emperor was clearly losing his authority over his men and finally he gave in to Ambrose. This submission was to be the prototype for the later submission of Henry IV, the German Emperor, to Pope Gregory VII at Canossa in 1077.

Theodosius later became a pupil of Ambrose, and under his tutelage, in 395, he abolished all the other religions of Rome and made Christianity the official religion of the state. This act brought the protest of the upper class, the intelligentsia of the empire, which was still largely pagan. Their protest centered about the removal of the statue of Fortuna from the senate hall, the market. For 800 years Rome had honored the God of Fortune and the intelligentsia appealed to no avail to the Emperor's sentiment to leave them this empty idol.

Theodosius was the last Roman-type ruler. His children were too young to rule and when he died were placed under the regency of the German, Stilicho, who assumed command. While Theodosius was being buried,

Ambrose made a speech in which he defined a new relationship between church and state. The Holy Roman Church was to engage in spiritual warfare with its goal being peace in Heaven; the Holy Roman Empire was to engage in physical warfare with its goal being peace on earth. These remarks were made about 395 A.D. In 410 A.D., Alaric, a disgruntled German who had been denied an expected promotion, organized a Roman-style army and sacked Rome. For 800 years Rome had lived under the pagan gods, and, just 15 years after the institution of the Christian God, Rome was sacked.

All around the shocked empire the question arose: Where was the Christian God? Why did he not protect Rome? The charge was made that when an Emperor turns Christian, it is all over with the state.

The church cast about to find someone who could answer the charges being leveled at it throughout the Empire, accusing it of being the cause of the sack of Rome.

It found such a man cultivated thoroughly in the pagan tradition in Augustine of Hippo, a philosopher who had been converted to Christianity by listening to Ambrose in Milan. St. Augustine was to play the same role to the Roman Empire that Polybius had played to the Roman republic, and which Plato and Aristotle had played to the Greek city-state.

Aristotle had defined the city-state as the chief instrument for the realization of a good life for man on earth. Polybius had tried to summarize what the Roman republic was capable of doing and what it needed to have to do it well. Both of these men had the misfortune of educating the very men who destroyed the things they were trying to preserve. Alexander the Great, the pupil of Aristotle, destroyed forever the possibility of the independent existence of the Greek city-state. Scipio, the pupil of Polybius, destroyed Carthage and with it the possibility of the existence of the Roman republic.

Augustine was given the opportunity to sum up the

meaning of the Roman empire while Boniface was about to destroy it. It was Boniface who admitted the barbarians. Procopius has observed that Aetius and Boniface have a right to be called the last of the Romans. Had these men lived in different times, separated from one another, Rome would have survived another 200 years or more. But they lived at the same moment in history and they did what Romulus and Remus had done. They fought it out. Boniface invited the Vandals in, and they took over North Africa. No longer would the Germans take orders from Rome. Out of the bitter rivalry between Aetius and Boniface, Rome came to an end.

Augustine is a fitting figure to stand at the end of the history of Rome. He answered the critics of the church, saying it was utterly false to say the Christians had weakened the empire. Contrasting the Christian and the pagan soldier, he held that the Christian soldier had served Rome the best. The vast majority of soldiers in the Roman legions, in proportion to the total population, had been Christians.

It was the decadence of Rome itself — its perpetual civil wars — that caused its downfall. The Roman characteristically had always fought for personal gain. The Christian had facilitated matters for Rome for he was taught to obey even a tyrant in battle; he was not fighting for personal interest.

Augustine then turned from the accusers of the church to the great majority of his readers who were Christians. Christianity, he said, will not save Rome. Christianity does not save states; it saves people.

Pilate had asked Jesus if he was a king and where his kingdom was. Jesus had replied that he was a king, but that his kingdom was not of this world. If it had been of this world, his servants would have raised their swords against Pilate.

Freud has observed that there are two forces operative in the world. Eros unites the world, but it is matched by a counter-force, aggression, which tends to cause separation. The great contribution of Augustine was that he conceived of those two forces as one force, Eros, or in the usage of St. Augustine, *cupiditas.*

Economic eros was greed. Sexual eros was desire. The philosophic eros was the avaricious desire to know. This was the sense in which the pagans had understood eros, as a force which attracts everything to self, which holds all the world together. Everything is pulled to its own place, attracted like filings to a magnet. The rock is pulled to the earth. The plant grows through self-nutrition. The animal, through sensation, animalizes its reproduction.

Man has sensation, which brings with it the appetites. The pagan observed that unfortunately the appetites get too big and they have to be regulated, but they cannot be regulated directly. A force can only be checked by another force; a will can only be balanced by another will. The appetites would consume everyone if they were left unchecked. All men desire to be happy and to live in peace. But they want to do this in their own way. So men struggle over a woman or they struggle over land. And the more truly they love peace, the more they will love it on their own terms, and the greater will be the occasion for war. The more ardent the love of man for peace, the more zealously will he hang those who oppose his will. Woe to the world when two sincere lovers of peace fight over it. The pursuit of peace is the maddest and wildest of straight jackets.

In St. Augustine's sense, cupiditas exists on all levels of being, and on all levels God lets it go unrestrained. But on the maximum level of power, that of the state, God out of his mercy sets up a counter will.

Augustine in *The City of God* calls attention to the proper way to maintain the goods of this world. The way is the way of Polybius and Aristotle. How far should a man defend his material interests, seeing that it will never be possible to charm out of human nature its fighting spirit? He must loose one power against another power.

There is only one politics, the politics of the damned where a self-destructive force is used to check a self-destructive force. There never has been a just state. Countering Cicero's belief that a state without justice will fall apart, St. Augustine tells the following anecdote. He refers to the meeting of Alexander the Great with a captured petty pirate. After Alexander had upbraided the man for his piracy, the pirate reminded Alexander that what he was doing on a small scale was what Alexander had been doing on a vast scale. On a large scale Alexander could not be caught and this gives way not to justice but to impunity.

The Marxian doctrine derives much of its appeal from its insight into the fact that all states are organized by bands of robbers that rob with impunity. What is the answer to this—a new state?

Augustine finished writing *The City of God* with the Vandals at the gates of Hippo. He died before Hippo was taken.

Athaulf, the successor of Alaric, at first intended to make Rome an Italic Gothic. But he perceived that the structure of Rome worked just as well when there were no Romans in charge of it. He decided instead to join Roman form with Gothic power.

Greek culture had conquered the conquering Roman, but the conquest by Roman law of the conquering German was far more thorough.

NOTES

1. There has been a trend among historians to find parallels between Oriental history and Western history. Some historians have even located a Chinese and an Indian Shakespeare.

Does the West think that it alone had a *pax romana*? The Orient had a *pax*, too. It seems to be the fashion to draw these kinds of parallels in modern history textbooks, but a truly great history of the Orient has yet to be written. The day that some historian forces Oriental history through the meat chopper of Polybius, as Roman history was forced, then, and only then, will the Orient have a history.

2. The other way to be honest would be to have a handsome reality and handsome laws. Most people have concluded it is best to be hypocritical and conceal ugly reality behind handsome laws, except those people who have the job of making a nation strong. The man who is concerned with his nation's strength does not ask of a law whether it is right and does not expect it to be handsome — but rather he asks if it is true to the realities with which it must deal. Should the Arabs, living in Israel, who would justifiably topple the Israeli nation given the chance, be governed in any other way except under Ben Gurian's military rule? Ben Gurian's ugly laws are realistic and in this respect he is a Roman, doubly ugly. Martin Buber would prefer handsome reality and handsome laws, but he doesn't have military control of a country.

Among friends hypocrisy is tolerance and good manners. You can't be frank, you must be polite. The decisions of our Supreme Court have caught the United States in a hypocritical pose. We have handsome laws but our reality is ugly. Most people in the U.S. know this.

3. It makes one wonder when in this day one hears so much about the desirability of cooperation among the armed forces, just how desirable inter-service cooperation really is. It is an

160

awesome thing when a commander is convinced that he can take the enemy all by himself, without the meddling of the other branches of the armed forces. It becomes even more awesome when the other branches have commanders who believe the same thing about themselves and are ready, if necessary, to prove it.

4. Recently, Prof. Richard Morris of Columbia expressed in an essay how offended he was by the U.S. symbol of the bald eagle. The bald eagle is a bird of prey. He suggests a less offensive bird would be more in keeping with our tradition. Possibly a bird is a bad symbol in the first place. Why not a dog — a tall, stately, proud, polite poodle?

5. When one considers the tremendous strain of a presidential campaign in the United States, one must conclude that whatever problems the president may be called upon to face after he has achieved office will seem to him like a restful vacation compared to the ordeal of winning the office.

Some political theorists have maintained that the hereditary monarchy is the most desirable form of government. This idea is not so ridiculous when one considers the function of the chief executive. The chief executive is primarily the man who signs a bill, thereby making it a law. Up to the moment that he affixes his signature to the bill, all parties are free to violently argue its pros and cons. But when the bill is signed, the argument is over. The opposing party must then face the fact that it has lost the argument, and that it is its duty to accept the law and uphold it with all its heart. The man who bears the attitude that although he lost he will keep on fighting the law which he does not want, has the wrong attitude. Any man who lives in a state subject to a law of which he does not consent, lives under a tyranny. Under our Constitution, the only way in which this tyranny can be avoided is to accept the rule of the majority, to identify the dissenting will with the majority will. It is the function of the Chief Executive to solemnize the moment when the bill becomes the law of the land. In a democracy, it is necessary that a man be in favor of what the majority wants, but it is also necessary that he remain free to try to persuade them to want something else.

In American politics, the defeated candidate, having heard the voice of the people, gracefully bows to his victorious opponent and promises to support him. This gesture on the part of the defeated candidate is necessary if the country is to move ahead, rationally and rapidly, but it does not prevent him from thinking of the next election.

Some political theorists feel that it would be far more rational, as in hereditary monarchy, to train a man from birth to do what must be done in that critical moment when many men must make a psychological flip in order to uphold the Constitution, when they must accept the majority will making it their own, and thereby provide that necessary unity which the Constitution requires.

6. We in the U.S. have very much this Roman spirit. That our country is largely held together by force is illustrated by the excessive stress placed on legality. The English do not need this binding cohesion of law so much because there is a pride in the significance of being an Englishman. The British state is bound together by the more than legal idea of what it means to be an Englishman. There is a tradition there which stimulates individual pride. What does it mean to be an American? It means primarily to have rights under the law, and to insist on these individual rights whether they are or are not shared by anyone else. This is not the best way to hold a society together. It is, in fact, the lowest common denominator because it tends like the Roman denominator to suppress. Our government like the Roman was technically founded on coercive power, which was intended to prevent an uprising of the powers of localized factions. Two things particularly did it try to suppress: monarchy and aristocracy. A lot of force was needed to do this. It was necessary to use the very institutions that were to be suppressed to prevent their emergence. We have to this day a secret aristocracy which Americans still conceal.

7. Rousseau had maintained that the land of the world belonged to everybody in the world, and that consequently none had a right to it. The arch villain, to Rousseau, was the man who set up boundaries. The Romans anticipated one had a right to the land of the world. But they also knew that the world and its land belonged to the man who could by his strength take it, and make the people he conquered respect the fact that he had taken it. Under Numa they proceeded to set up their boundaries.

8. We really know more about early Rome than about early Greece. But what we know about Rome has been subjected to a

much more severe criticism. The Roman legends are comparable in significance to the Homeric stories of the Greeks, but they are not as well defended by art. What the dates of the incidents in these legends were, or whether they happened at all, can never be proved.

The legends of early Rome and the systematic historical thinking they have suggested have all been subjected to skeptical criticism. But if one wants to reject a system of historical thought that makes these stories meaningful, he must also reject the stories. The only remedy for skepticism, and the only defense against it, is to have a system in one's thinking.

If the system builder builds well, then any part of his system will necessarily depend on the rest. His skeptical critic may reject the whole construction — but if he should happen to accept just one small point in the system, he would then be forced by logic to accept the rest.

A defense of a construction, such as that of Polybius or Hegel against skepticism, should not be direct. Skepticism is never answered directly. The construction is its own defense.

If the skeptic chooses to question not the system itself, but the personal motives or mental idiosyncrasy of the individual who created the system, the best rebuttal is to ask the skeptic what *his* personal motives are that make him so skeptical of the motives of another.

It is perfectly all right to criticize or reject altogether Polybius or Hegel or for that matter all system builders, but should the skeptic choose to do this, he should be reminded that it is not easy to *not* believe anything, and that to do this competently he must build a whole system of thought himself.

The skeptic cannot have a whole world of disorder and at the same time keep a little raft of order all for himself. The dilemma of the skeptic is the dilemma of Hamlet. The ghost comes to Hamlet and says "justify me." But how can Hamlet do this when the whole world is out of joint? How can he do the right thing when nothing is right?

One cannot think this way. Either save everything or save nothing. Is the world and its history meaningful? Either it is and from the beginning has been meaningful, or there is not and never was any meaning.

There are two ways of thinking about patterns in history. The first way is employed by most historians. They reject a belief in patterns and proceed to follow a pattern in arranging their material. The second way is to honestly accept the patterns history follows as real and as obviously of a type susceptible to scientific treatment. It is only necessary to ask the historian who rejects belief in patterns, "How did you arrange your facts?" It is unlikely that anyone has ever approached history by studying everything that simultaneously happened in 509.

Chronology alone does not determine pattern. The modern world feels closer in time to the ancient world than to the medieval world. How a story is told will determine its shape.

9. It is characteristic of all revolutions that at the outset the entire people is aligned against the common enemy. The communists usually utilize the services of the anarchist and liberal intellects in the preliminary phases of revolution. But after the revolution is won, these people must be gotten rid of, since the very philosophies which made them useful revolutionaries make them a menace to the newly formed state.

After the American Revolution, when the United States had established itself on high principles, any subordinate revolution or dissension from these principles, as with the southern states, was smashed. In the beginning of the revolution it was necessary to get everyone on the American side. The revolutionaries ranged from the permanent revolutionary, Thomas Paine, whose philosophy might be condensed to the statement "wherever freedom is not, there is my home," to the pacifist, Franklin, whose philosophy might be "wherever freedom is, there is my home." But when a revolution is over, the permanent revolutionary is out of place, and while the aristocrats begin to conserve again, he must seek out new revolutions.

10. In our day the people who cut coupons worry about how to induce the lower classes to adopt some more effective method of birth control, which will reduce the rate of their reproduction, while they try to devise new ways to placate the masses that are left with the benefits that taxation makes possible. There are only two things a coupon cutter can do; he can either keep the masses away or be brave.

11. The "two consul system" of Rome was a well thought out scheme. With it, executive power was held, however imperfectly, within some bounds.

The obvious corruption to which an executive office is susceptible sometimes makes one overlook its other possibilities. The executive does provide leadership even if it is at a dangerous price. Unlike Rome, where the consul enjoyed his power for one year, in Florence executives were changed every two months. It was a period just long enough for an executive to provide some leadership to the state and aggrandizement for himself.

If one wants the leadership of an executive, one must be prepared to risk danger. Freedom has always been identified with the danger of tyranny. And tyranny would have always followed as two consuls approached the end of their terms, if Rome had not held over their heads the potential office of dictator which could override both of them.

12. When trivial offenses are subject to capital punishment, then inevitably those trivial offenses are eliminated from the society. A man will abstain from purse snatching when he knows he will get the chair for it. There is only one thing capital punishment cannot eliminate, and that is deliberate murder. The man who deliberately kills wants to go to the chair. If his sentence was not the chair and he shared the same punishment as men who committed lesser crimes, he could be righteously indignant.

It takes courage to want to go to the chair. If the death penalty for murder is ever abolished, the suicide rate among convicted murderers will be very high.

If the death penalty were abolished, the murderer would demand it be re-established. He needs it to justify his having killed another man. For when he kills he is doing two things, and doing them willingly and deliberately. He is killing his victim and he is sentencing himself to death.

The payment for his crime with his life rationalizes the act as well as the law under which it was committed.

But it requires a rational state to sanction a law such as this. This kind of legal rationalism treats the criminal as if he were a man who was responsible. To be equal means to be equally responsible.

Even if everyone tries to persuade the man that he was not responsible, as the psychologists would, he should insist on his right to be recognized as responsible.

13. The Franciscans tried to do away with private property, by sharing things in common among themselves as well as among the larger community. It remains that they had to retain certain

things which necessarily belonged to them.

Is property essential to man?

The Greeks believed that reason was the essential quality of man. Reason made possible a trait which, though not essential to man, characterized him. This was his ability to smile. In the entire animal kingdom, which lacks reason, there is not one creature that can even begin to smile. It is no trivial thing that a smile is characteristic of man alone. The smile expresses the diminution of the animal nature by reason. It is characteristic, though not essential, to man.

Property is not essential to man. It is something that belongs to him and can be severed from him without destroying his essential nature, but just as a smile, it characterizes him.

Ownership of property is just a relation between human and inanimate things. No one could abolish ownership except by canceling out all the laws of a society. The actual relations between a human being and a thing determines whether the human being owns that thing.

14. If a man doesn't care about the commonwealth of which he owns nothing, should he have as much to say about what happens to it as the man who does care because he is deeply involved in it? Such a man should not have much to say.

A state where the citizens have an equal voice in the government but have different shares of the commonwealth is a facade government. A man can have an equal voice with other men only about those things which he owns equally with them. The United States has been a facade government. Now it is on the verge of becoming a popular dictatorship, that is to say, a dictatorship with the absolute consent of the people in which the dictator does away with the intermediate classes that separate him from the people. Who really believes that a democracy is operated by the banner of the French Revolution, by liberty, equality and fraternity?

When men seriously pursue an end and value it highly, they will not take into their group the man who contributes nothing. If an end is really valued, men will ask each other, "what is your share in this?"

The lower classes can gain only when the nobles split up among themselves or when the extraordinary noble, who does not think the nobles are noble enough, aligns himself with the masses.

The greatest benefactor to equality is the man who is so high above the people that he can afford to laugh at their differences. No one else can do this. In this area there has been such a falsification of history on the part of historians who are primarily concerned with being allowed to live in their age, that our learning has become Byzantine.

15. The censor's office began merely as an excuse for relieving the executive of tedious paperwork. What happened in Rome is in no way different from what happens in our country.

How much can a president really do by himself? He is dependent on his servile paper workers. In order to find out what is going on in the country, he has to ask the men who keep the papers. The paper worker has an awesome power. He is the only man who knows which papers are important. The situation has gotten to the point where the real business of running the government is carried on by the anonymous paper worker, while the chief executive's office has declined to the dispensable function of entertaining visiting dignitaries and boy-scout troops.

16. Rousseau wrote a celebrated treatise on how the common will is formed. His treatment of the problem is meaningless unless it is realized that all states have always been faced with the same problem. The Romans worked out the problem little by little in practice, as opposed to Rousseau's theoretical approach.

The problem is to get men to submit equally to a state and thereby create a common will. What if we had 100 men and wanted to create a common will among them? Would it be equal submission if they all gave one dollar toward the common will? Suppose one man who gave one dollar only had two dollars, and another who gave one dollar had one thousand. There would be an unequal submission here, since one man gave half of his earnings and another one thousandth. What if everybody gave half of his earnings? Now one man would give one dollar to 500 dollars of the other. But this would still leave one man with one dollar and the other with $500. They would obviously not have submitted equally, since the man with $500 would still have a substantial margin of private wealth. The remedy for this might be something like our graduated income tax where the upper brackets submit 91% of their earnings. But would this create a common will? The man who gives 90% is being left with 10%, is left with a million dollars, which could easily grow more millions. Has he submitted equally?

Rousseau's solution to the problem was to have everybody give 100% to the common will. Everybody gives everything to the common will and is credited for having given it.

The culmination of the problem was reached with Robespierre who granted that everybody had given everything to the common will, but then he asked the big question. Did they really want to give it? What about the interior will?

When a man begins to question the interior will, he inaugurates a "reign of suspicion." It becomes then a discussion of whether a man was really willing to have willed the common will. Robespierre scrutinized everybody and found that nobody was willing but Robespierre. Since Robespierre was the only one willing, it became obviously necessary to get rid of him, just as it was necessary to get rid of Cromwell. After Robespierre was disposed of, a truly marvelous moment in history was reached when nobody was willing to do what nobody wills, and nothing got done until somebody was willing again.

Immanuel Kant, in his *Critique of Practical Reason*, pointed out that to be willing to will what one wills is the source of all right.

But, is there not another will somewhere that makes one want to will something else? This other will shows on the face of our statesmen. To put it differently, their heads are convinced but their hearts are not. And this is the source of all wrong. Kant was perfectly correct.

The basic thing that is happening in the world today is an effort to condemn the private will. If a man insists on disagreeing with the common will, the only logical thing to do with him, according to Rousseau, is to remove him from the area of influence. But, if he disagrees with one common will, he will doubtless disagree with all the others. There is no room for him to exist between the boundaries of two common wills. So he will be squeezed out of existence in that spaceless area where two common wills grind against each other to form a boundary. He will, in a word, be exterminated. France, under Napoleon, had achieved a common will. Russia to this day has not achieved it. It is still largely despotic and will have to go through an entire devolution of power. The passage from Stalin to Khruschev has been from despotism to oligarchy. Khruschev is himself limited by it. He is fond of pointing out that no man should have all the power in his hands. The man who says this, however, is the man who frequently has all the power in his hands because no other man is permitted to have it.

17. The distinction between the patricians and the plebeians ended with the Battle of Orders, when the plebs secured the right to occupy seats of government. The distinction thereafter is used only metaphorically.

18. It cannot be said that this decision was inevitable. After a decision is made and its consequences have run their course, it is easy for later historians to see the inevitability of the choice out of all the choices that were possible. Rome's decision to come to the aid of the Mamartines might be thought of in Rostovtzeff's sense as a pretext with a broader aim in view.

But there is no assurance that the Romans felt the inevitability or necessity of their actions.

As Immanuel Kant has pointed out, two things never change: the law which moves the stars and the human will which doubts the laws. Necessity may be an iron law which causes the atoms to bump together in certain ways, but when they bump together to form man, they produce a creature who is able to deny the need of necessity. The truly great thinkers have resolved this dilemma by defining freedom as the "insight into necessity."

19. The man who is victorious in battle and has his enemy pinned to the ground can either run him through or let him get up again. Should he choose to let him up, he can ask the man whose life he has spared, "What do I owe you?" To this the defeated can only answer one thing: "Nothing." He can further ask, What do you owe me?" Again there is only one reply, "My life." This situation is the source of slavery.

MacArthur did not meet the representatives of a defeated Japan to discuss the terms of surrender; these had been decided in battle. All he wanted from them was their signatures.

Imposing unconditional surrender on the enemy, as we did with Germany and Japan, or as the Jews did with the Arabs, is identical with pinning a man into helplessness in battle, and whether the vanquished is a nation or an individual, they are reduced to the same condition, slavery. Whatever life they may enjoy after their surrender, they enjoy as a gift from their conqueror; and the condition of freedom prior to their defeat can never again be reconstructed.

20. What is the difference between force and law? If a man is sent to jail by force, he is being imprisoned without his consent. If he is sent to jail by law, he is being imprisoned with his consent.

Law needs force but it also needs authority. Authority is attained by law only when the person over whom a law is enforced gives his consent.

Is authority a desirable quality? Do rulers really want it? They want it more than anything else in the world. With authority a ruler can do tremendous things, for his subjects willingly obey. Without authority the ruler must use a mercenary to push his unwilling subjects from behind.

21. There is no way of overlooking the hard fact that these distinctions apply today. War has put an end to man's natural state of freedom. Man's original state of freedom has been forever lost in the victories and defeats that all peoples have endured. And this freedom cannot be recaptured by abolishing the laws of nations.

The Romans spoke very distinctly about the rights of man but they never defined what a man was. They did define a slave, but he could be made a man by a very slight adjustment.. In our country, because we had defined both man and slave, it required a tremendous upheaval to make a slave a man.

The United States has a natural law constitution; therefore, it defines too much. The British have refused to have a natural law constitution. By leaving their rights undefined, they have made it difficult for them to be taken away.

British common law is a great protector of rights, resting as it does on precedents that can be pushed back a thousand years. The only place a question of rights can be settled is in court. Once in court, a massive process is begun which has to sift through a millennium of precedents.

Genuine freedom means to have an infinitude of obligations so that no one of them can be enslaving. This was the meaning of Anglo-Saxon freedom. The French Revolution wiped out this kind of freedom in France.

22. It was a kind of shadow cabinet which resembles what we find in England today. In England all functions of state in detail are carried on by two governments, the party in power and the opposition party. The Queen has even authorized that all knowledge of state affairs be shared with the shadow government. This

is calculated to avert what in our country is a great disaster. When a party retires from power, it is replaced by men who are totally uninformed of the actual affairs of state. When a shift in power occurs in our government, there is this dangerous interval when the next party has to find out what has really been going on.

23. It was the "luck of the Romans" that no one took advantage of the many opportunities to attack Rome while her armies were preoccupied in other lands. All her foreign wars seemed to be synchronized so that she was always called upon to start a new war, only after she had finished an old one. This military policy ran the risk of great danger, but the Romans used to say that great nations take chances.

24. The "Lives" of Plutarch are rich with wonderful moments such as when he describes the time Pompey and Crassus came back to Rome and decided to run for election together. This would be like Barry Goldwater running on the same ticket with John Kennedy. People were alarmed. What were they trying to do? Somebody had to oppose them, and yet no one was too anxious to do it. Cato pushed an opposing candidate forward.

Cato had great influence and the candidate could have caused trouble. So Pompey and Crassus dispatched a band of thugs to beat up the candidate. At the approach of the thugs, all the people fled except the indomitable Cato who restrained his candidate from fleeing, forcing him to be courageous in spite of himself.

25. This extract is typical of the style of Cicero in which sentence piles upon sentence by a steady repetition of rhythm, building in force, until the suspense is climaxed by a smashing torrent of words.

There is great power in words. But there are only certain times in history when this power works. Genuine rhetoric can flourish only in the third and final phase of the devolution of power, when the populace is on the verge of being the arbiter. Rhetoric does not hold sway in an aristocratic assembly.

Aristotle says that in a court of law, where one should want to learn the truth, rhetoric is out of place. In an aristocratic assembly the greatest rhetorician could be made to appear ridiculous with the greatest ease.

26. An instance of a practical application of Caesar's attitude was Bismarck. His great task was to deprive Austria of the leadership

of Germany. So he very coldly threw his support to Prussia; and allowing her to pursue her policies, Austria, furious, consequently became engaged in a war against Bismarck, after she and Prussia had previously been involved in a war over Denmark. But in the last stages of the war of 1866 as Austria faced certain defeat at Bismarck's hands, to the dismay of the Kaiser, Bismarck called a halt and suggested they come to terms. The Kaiser was inconsolable. Why come to terms when an unconditional surrender could have been forced on Austria? Bismarck not only came to terms, but he gave Austria extremely generous terms, at the same time eliminating Austria from any influence in German affairs.

To the Kaiser he explained that it is true that it would be right to prostrate Austria, but the question of right was not at issue. The big question was not whether one wants right or wrong, but whether one wants a united Germany.

It was this kind of coldness that Caesar was suggesting.

27. Everything he prophesied was correct up to this point. But here he seems to go wrong.

In Hebraic tradition the Augustan age was called the fullness of time. An incredible transformation occurred in the Greco-Roman attitude to oriental religions, particularly the Hebraic. There was a longing for salvation, for help, for an Eden, for the golden past. And it arose spontaneously throughout the Roman Empire.

Polybius foresaw only a master and a despot.

28. Mussolini perceived that the dissension of party factions weakened the state. Believing that to maintain internal order there must be a unifying principle above party factions, he resurrected the old Roman principle that what pleases the first officer of the nation has the force of law. When he first uttered this principle, it was a dizzying concept with awesome implications, and he dreamed of a resurrected Roman Empire. But someone wryly remarked in the Italian parliament that Mussolini could please what he wished, but if it pleases Germany, she could walk through Italy in three days and, if she cared to, take Sicily on the fourth.

When can a man make such a statement and not be utterly ridiculous? Only when there is no other force in the world that might choose to oppose on the battlefield that which pleases the first officer.

29. The recent United States disarmament proposal, which was happily rejected, proposed that the United Nations should have greater military power than all its members. What was the United States aiming at? Was it not a situation that had been achieved by the principate of Rome?

How is it with the United Nations in reality? If it proposes something which is pleasing to its members, they back it with power. Otherwise, they do not.

But in order to effectively confer such suggested absolute power upon the UN, it would have to be granted beforehand, not only on those occasions when what the UN pleases to do satisfies its members. The power would have to be acknowledged ahead of time, and the risk taken that the decisions of the UN would be satisfactory, though they might just as easily not be satisfactory. The United States peace proposal is something to think about. Rome had achieved it. It had established a world government dedicated to the principle of equality. It had passed through three stages: the first stage, where there were no foreign entanglements, the stage of civil strife; the second stage, when it set up its Monroe Doctrine; and the final stage, where it went out to make the world safe for democracy — and succeeded.

Every nation passes to some extent through these stages. Even modern Israel went through a formative stage, where it concentrated on its civil laws and then proclaimed to all nations that no one was to invade Israel, and finally decided not to wait to be invaded but sent out its forces beyond its boundaries, feeling it was better to hit the enemy first.

The British intentionally did not follow this course but deliberately kept their enemy, Germany, free. They knew that the divided sovereignty which is necessary for freedom requires the presence of an enemy.

30. The only nation in the west that seems to perceive this truth is Italy. The Italians would agree that it is necessary to do dreadful things to save the constitution; in fact, they are eager to do them even before they are necessary. Italy is teeming with little Machiavellis.

31. Maitland observes that England was the only European nation that did not adopt Roman law, escaping thereby the fate which paralyzed the continent.

England does not subscribe to natural reason as a criterion for legal matters, and it has a good chance to survive because of this. In America, as a recent Supreme Court decision reveals, reason is the predominating criterion of law. With respect to law it is possible to be either a rationalist or a nationalist.

An honest, upright rationalist would maintain that what is good for America is good for every nation in the world. A nationalist would never say this. He would say that what is good for America is bad for the rest of the world.

Justice Frankfurter, in his recent Supreme Court decision, spoke in the manner of a Roman lawyer in words that even Cicero could not surpass, when he observed that our courts derived their authority neither from the purse, nor the sword, but from the confidence of the people. To maintain this confidence, they must remain above factional interests. The only criterion that the courts can employ if they are to achieve the impartiality Frankfurter describes, is the disinterested reason of Roman Law.

32. But then they lost the state. The Romans picked up the torch and chose to protect the state at any cost. They flung out buffer after buffer around it, to preserve it, and they did this with such inevitable depressing concentration of power that men finally began to listen, when the Jews started talking about God again.